Baker College of  RV

D1081865

THE EUROPEAN UNION AND THE ARAB SPRING

THE EUROPEAN UNION AND THE ARAB SPRING

Promoting Democracy and Human Rights in the Middle East

Edited by Joel Peters

LEXINGTON BOOKS
Lanham • Boulder • New York • Toronto • Plymouth, UK

Published by Lexington Books
A wholly owned subsidiary of The Rowman & Littlefield Publishing Group,
Inc.
4501 Forbes Boulevard, Suite 200, Lanham, Maryland 20706
www.lexingtonbooks.com

Estover Road, Plymouth PL6 7PY, United Kingdom

Copyright © 2012 by Lexington Books

All rights reserved. No part of this book may be reproduced in any form or
by any electronic or mechanical means, including information storage and
retrieval systems, without written permission from the publisher, except by a
reviewer who may quote passages in a review.

British Library Cataloguing in Publication Information Available

Library of Congress Cataloging-in-Publication Data

The European Union and the Arab Spring : promoting democracy and human
rights in the Middle East / [edited by] Joel Peters.
    p. cm.
  Includes bibliographical references and index.
  ISBN 978-0-7391-7443-2 (cloth : alk. paper) — ISBN 978-0-7391-7445-6 (pbk. :
alk. paper) — ISBN 978-0-7391-7444-9 (electronic)
  1. European Union countries—Foreign relations—Middle East. 2. Middle
East—Foreign relations—European Union countries. 3. Middle East—Politics
and government—21st century. 4. Middle East—Social conditions—21st century. 5. Democratization—Middle East. I. Peters, Joel.
  JZ1570.A55E979 2012
  327.4056090512—dc23   2011049545

Printed in the United States of America

∞ ™ The paper used in this publication meets the minimum requirements
of American National Standard for Information Sciences—Permanence of Paper for Printed Library Materials, ANSI/NISO Z39.48-1992.
Printed in the United States of America

Contents

Acknowledgments

Many friends and colleagues have contributed to the making of this book. First I would like to thank all the authors of the book, not only for their contributions but responding to my constant emails and ensuring that the manuscript was completed on time. This has been truly a collective effort.

Earlier drafts of the chapters were first discussed at a workshop organized by the Forum on the Problems of Peace and War, Florence on 24 September 2011. I would like to thank Sonia Lucarelli and Lorenzo Fioramonti and all the staff of the Forum for organizing that workshop. George Christou, Michela Ceccorulli, Stuart Croft, Sonia Lucarelli, Alberto Tonini, and Valeria Talbot all offered important feedback on those early drafts at that workshop, and encouraged us to go forward and publish the papers.

The workshop and this book is an outcome of a research consortium EU-GRASP (www.eugrasp.eu), a collaborative research project funded by the Seventh Framework Programme of the European Commission (FP7/2007-2013- grant agreement n° 225722). The consortium has been addressing the role of the European Union as a peace and security actor within the context of a changing multilateral environment for the past three years. EU-GRASP has been a wonderful combination of rigorous scholarship, frank exchange of ideas, and strong collegial friendships.

I would also like to thank two close friends who were not directly involved in this project, Claire Spencer and Sharon Pardo. Claire and I have been discussing Europe's relations in the Middle East since the early days of the Barcelona Process. That process may have withered but our friendship has gone from strength to strength. Claire deserves special credit for keeping me (and my family) sane during the final days of completing this book. Sharon Pardo, my co-author on my two previous books with Lexington Books, *Uneasy Neighbors: Israel and the European Union* (2010) and *Israel and the European Union: A Documentary History* (2012), has been a constant source of advice and support. His friendship, especially over the past three years, is deeply appreciated. I would also like to extend my support to my friends and (former) colleagues in the Department of Politics and Government at Ben Gurion University for their work in promoting a greater understanding of human rights and democracy within Israel. I am proud to have been a founder member of the department and to have played a part in those efforts.

Susan Kennedy copyedited the manuscript with her usual efficiency and exceptional skill. Over the years, Susan has been a source of good spirit and friendship, way beyond making my prose more legible. Thanks also to Molly Mallon, my research assistant at Virginia Tech for checking all the chapters, notes, and bibliography, and for making sure the final version of the manuscript was ready on time.

Lenore Lautigar at Lexington Books deserves special mention. This is my third book with Lexington and my second working directly with Lenore. An exchange of emails prior to the Florence workshop turned within days into a book proposal, and then a contract. Working with Lenore (and all the staff at Lexington Books) is simply a great pleasure—she combines a quiet efficiency with a warm personal touch.

None of this would be at all possible without the love and support of my wife, Sandra and my sons, Gabe and Ari. Together, they give meaning to everything I do. And finally, my dog Muki who has sat under my desk for the past twelve years, has heard more about Europe's relations with the Middle East than any dog should suffer.

Joel Peters
November 2011

A note on terminology: This book looks at the policies of the European Union toward North Africa and the Middle East. At times, the term Europe is used as a generic term for the European Union (EU), its institutions, and member states. Under the 1992 Treaty on European Union (the Maastricht Treaty) the European Community (EC) was included under the new structure of the EU. For brevity, throughout the book, we generally refer to the EU despite legal distinctions between the EC and the EU.

Introduction

Europe and the Challenge of the Arab Spring

Joel Peters

On 17 December 2010 Mohammed Buazizi, a Tunisian fruit and vegetable seller, set himself on fire after the police confiscated his cart. Buazizi's act of self-immolation led to a series of demonstrations across the country accompanied by strikes and acts of civil resistance. At first, the protests in Tunisia drew little international attention. The Tunisian police and security forces failed to quell the wave of popular unrest and the crisis continued to escalate between 8–12 January 2011 with further violent encounters between the police and demonstrators. On 14 January Tunisian President Zine El Abdine Ben Ali declared a state of emergency and fired his cabinet. By the end of the day, however, Ben Ali had fled the country.

The Tunisian protests and the fall of Ben Ali's regime captured the popular imagination and spawned a wave of uprisings across North Africa and the Middle East which the Western media dubbed "the Arab Spring." Demanding political reform and economic freedom, the protestors swept away the authoritarian autocratic regimes of the Middle East.

Inspired by events in Tunisia, the Egyptian people took to the streets at the end of January calling for the resignation of President Hosni Mubarak, who eventually handed over power on 11 February. In Libya, the protests led to a six-month civil war and the overthrow of Colonel Gaddafi's regime, and to his capture and death at the hands of the Libyan opposition forces. The uprisings have also led to violent clashes between the demonstrators and the police and security forces, most notably in Syria, Bahrain, and Yemen whose regimes sought to suppress calls for reform and particularly the use of force. In Syria, the crackdown on public dissent by the armed forces has led to an estimated 5,000 civilian deaths over the past year and has resulted in the imposition of a series of economic and political sanctions on Syria by the United States, the European Union and the Arab League, and to calls for Syrian President Bashar Assad to carry out real reforms or leave office.

The events of the Arab Spring have been historic. They have led to profound changes in the domestic order of Middle Eastern states and societies. The Arab Spring has also impacted on the international politics of the region and will necessitate a comprehensive reappraisal by the United States and most notably by the EU of their relations with the states and peoples of the region.

This book looks at the response of the European Union to the Arab Spring. The chapters in this book pose three questions: What role did the European Union play in promoting democracy and human rights in the countries of North Africa and the Middle East; how did the European Union respond to the uprisings of the Arab street; and what are the challenges now facing Europe in its relations with the region in light of the Arab Spring?

Given its geographical proximity to the Middle East, as well as its historical legacy and economic, political and cultural ties with the region, the European Union has a longstanding interest in the Middle East. Over the past two decades, the European Union has made the promotion of human rights and democracy a central platform in the development of its relations with the Middle East. The 1995 Euro-Mediterranean Partnership (Barcelona Process) sought to strengthen the role of civil society in the southern Mediterranean states and to encourage the promotion of democracy and human rights, while building a sustainable and balanced economy and civil society in the region. The European Neighbourhood Policy (ENP), introduced in 2004, built on this platform. The promotion of democracy and respect for human rights were presented as core values shaping the EU's external action in non-EU countries. ENP Action Plans, which were jointly agreed between the EU and each non-EU country, noted that the pace of progress in the development of relations would be determined by "a state's commitment to values such as the rule of law, good governance, respect for human rights, and the promotion of good neighborly relations."[1]

Yet, despite this professed support for the promotion of civil society and human rights, the policies and actions of the European Union (or to be more precise the absence of policies) had no influence on the Arab Spring or the revolutions of the past year. As Štephan Füle, the Commissioner responsible for Enlargement and European Neighbourhood Policy, acknowledged: "We must show humility about the past. Europe was not vocal enough in defending human rights and local democratic forces in the region."[2] Through their silence, and their support of authoritarian regimes in the Middle East, European states became acquiescent in the suppression of human rights and freedoms.

The gap between rhetoric and practice in European policies in the Middle East is a theme common in all the chapters in this book. Human rights and the promotion of democratic reform ultimately lost out to a more urgent and competing set of European priorities in the region. The need for stability and security soon emerged as key drivers of the European Neighbourhood Policy, topping Europe's agenda and overshadowing principles of democratic reform and human rights.

In particular, the European Union saw the ruling Arab regimes as vital allies against the rise of Islamic radicalism, especially in the years after 9/11. European leaders were fearful that open and accelerated democratic reform would result in fundamentalist Islamic parties taking power. As Jean-Pierre Cassarino notes in his chapter, before the Arab Spring, dissent and genuine political opposition were viewed as a potential threat to "stability," not only by political elites and regimes of the Middle East, but also by European leaders. The violent repression of political dissent was thus often met with silent acquiescence by European elites.

The promotion of human rights has also played second fiddle to Europe's need to co-opt North African regimes to control the flow of illegal migration, and to protect vested European economic interests throughout the region, most notably in the Gulf countries. As Tobias Schumacher points out, commercial interests, the need for investment from the capital-rich Gulf countries, and, above all, the desire of France and the United Kingdom (and other European countries) to secure lucrative multi-billion dollar arms deals with the GCC countries, has over-ridden all other policy considerations towards those countries.

The prioritization of stability, fear of political Islam and need to protect its economic interests led to a reluctance on the part of the European Union to push Arab leaders on the question of human rights and democratic reform. Displaying (over)confidence in the capacity of the European Union as a normative power to project its values and principles beyond its borders, European leaders believed that democratic reform would emerge through a combination of repeated interaction, political dialogue and economic incentives. Such an approach, however, underestimated the adaptive resilience of Arab regimes and overestimated the willingness of Arab leaders to engage in serious dialogue over reform. As the European Commission admitted, their dialogues with officials in Mediterranean non-EU countries did not result in any discussions of substance. Instead they served as "a pretext for avoiding serious discussions on issues of human rights and democratic reforms in Mediterranean countries."[3]

The reality was that European policy towards the region prior to the Arab uprisings was a victory of pragmatism and vested interest over principle. But this approach was guided by the misguided belief that authoritarian regimes and autocratic leaders were the best guarantees of stability in the region. As Štephan Füle admitted: "This was not even Realpolitik. It was, at best, short-termism—and the kind of short-termism that makes the long term ever more difficult to build."[4]

The Arab uprisings and the pace at which events developed clearly caught European leaders by surprise. In May 2010 the EU and Tunisia had begun negotiations towards upgrading the latter's status within the ENPI to "advanced status."[5] At the time Štephan Füle stated that EU-Tunisian relations were "excellent," and described Tunisia as "an important and reliable partner" and an "economic pioneer among European Union neighbours."[6] The European Union was slow to respond to events. It was not until 10 January that it responded to the demonstrations in Tunisia and surprisingly, as Marco Pinfari notes, by supporting Ben Ali and announcing that negotiations to upgrade relations with Tunisia would continue, but now with a greater emphasis on human rights and fundamental freedoms. Four days later, Ben Ali was gone from power.

As the peoples across the Middle East took to the streets, the EU was cautious and low-key in its response and level of support. In a European Parliament debate on 2–3 February, 2011, EU foreign policy chief, Catherine Ashton, delivered a bland, and underwhelming statement: "As the European Union, our offer to the region and its people is solidarity and support to put reforms in place. The EU is a union of democracies—we have a democratic calling. So we will back this process of change, with patience, creativity and determination."[7] In response to the crackdown by Bahraini security forces, the EU called "on all parties to exercise restraint and calm" and "to engage rapidly in meaningful dialogue with a view to bringing about reforms which offer real prospects for successfully addressing the country's challenges,"[8] though it failed to define the nature of the reforms needed or the challenges facing Bahrain.

The violence in Libya and Syria created a different set of challenges for the European Union. In the case of Libya, the EU member states found themselves at odds over the question of military intervention in the support of the rebel forces. From the outset of the crisis, France and the United Kingdom pushed for a more forceful collective European response, while other members, notably Germany and Italy, held back and preferred a more cautious response.

The EU's failure to take the lead in managing the Libyan crisis, and its inability to respond in a timely, decisive, effective and unified fashion, is seen by many as reflective of its ineffectiveness to serve as a collective security actor. In the case of Syria, as

Carin Berg shows, the European Union was surprisingly quiet during the initial months, effectively acting as an observer to the escalating violence and mounting death toll. It was not until the summer that the European Union found its voice, leading efforts at the UN Security Council for sanctions to be imposed on Syria. After failing to secure the support of Russia and China, the EU has acted unilaterally over the past few months and imposed a progressively more restrictive set of sanctions on Syria to deter the Syrian government from resorting to violence and to pressure it to embark on dialogue and reform. In September, EU foreign ministers imposed an embargo on the importing and transporting of Syrian crude oil and petroleum, a measure likely to have a deleterious impact on the Syrian economy. But the EU has refrained so far from entering into any serious discussions on more forceful measures, in particular the possibility of military intervention in response to the repressive actions of the Syrian regime.

At the beginning of March, the EU expressed its support for the transformations in the Middle East by proposing a "Partnership for Democracy and Shared Prosperity with the Southern Mediterranean,"[9] which reframed existing policies based on a more proactive approach to economic and political reforms, democracy and social justice. This was followed in May by the publication of a review by the European Neighborhood Policy which offered a new approach aimed at "strengthen[ing] the partnership between the EU and the countries and societies of the neighborhood: to build and consolidate healthy democracies, pursue sustainable economic growth and manage cross-border links."[10] As part of this new approach an additional 1.24 billion Euros was made available on top of the 5.7 billion Euros already allocated for the period 2011–2013 in support of the ENP. Moreover, the European Council agreed to increase the lending envelope of the European Investment Bank (EIB) by 1 billion Euros, enabling the EIB to lend almost 6 billion Euros to the southern Mediterranean countries during the same period. The increase in ENPI budget lines was, however, conditional on the fulfillment of certain expectations. For example, the new Tunisian government was charged with taking effective action to curb illegal immigration to European countries (see chapter by Pinfari in this volume).

For many, there is little new in this "more funds for more reform approach." As Michele Pace argues, financial assistance was deemed the answer to the upheavals and democratic aspirations of peoples of the region, with no mention within the new initiative as to how the EU was actually going to support the development of "deep democracy" in its southern neighborhood. Furthermore, as Oz Hassan points out, the emphasis on partnership, gradualism and economic liberalization is significantly different from the demands of the Tahrir Square protestors, whose concept of freedom was articulated with human rights, social justice and in some significant quarters adherence to an Islamic framing rather than economic prosperity.

The current reframing of the European Neighborhood Policy places great emphasis on the role to be played by civil society in the transition to new forms of governance structures. The EU stressed that a new partnership with local societies would be implemented with a view to reinforcing the advocacy capacity of civil society organizations (CSOs) and non-governmental organizations (NGOs) in the region. These organizations would have access to EU funds through the creation of a Civil Society Facility and through the establishment of the European Endowment for Democracy, which would assist political parties, NGOs, trade unions and other social organizations. At the same time, Jean-Pierre Cassarino cautions, such CSO-friendly initiatives may in fact reflect a desire to control civil society actors through managed (and manageable) channels of communication between government officials and CSOs, and through the selective allocations of EU funds. The European Union needs to be open to all voices from the region, especially to those that do not share Europe's priorities and concerns and which present a different concept of democracy and the role of religion in the public sphere. Moreover, the new Civil Society Facility should be established with the full participation of Arab civil society organizations and not designed exclusively in Brussels, which might be out of touch with the region's needs.

Paradoxically, at a time when Arab civil society is finally able to express itself, the Israeli government, as discussed in the chapter by Joel Peters, is enacting legislation which undermines the activities, freedom of expression and funding of Israeli human rights and other civil society organizations. The European Union needs to affirm the importance of freedom of speech, and the role civil society organizations play in cementing the foundations of free, open and pluralistic societies. In fact the EU needs to go beyond expressing solidarity with those organizations currently under attack in Israel and maintain, if not increase, its financial support of those Israeli human rights and civil society organizations. It should also seek ways to develop new networks and foster the conditions for dialogue between Israeli and Arab civil society organizations beyond the specificity of the Arab-Israeli conflict.

The Arab Spring will require from the European Union a re-evaluation of its relationship with Islam and its engagement with Islamic political parties. A theme highlighted throughout this book is that European policy towards the Middle East has been driven in part by a fear of Islam and the rise of Islamic radicalism. As a consequence the EU distanced itself and, in certain places, refused to engage in dialogue with Islamic political parties or offer any support to Islamic civil society organizations. Such a monolithic framing of Islam is no longer possible, as the electoral success of the Islamist party An-Nahda in the Tunisian elections at the end of October 2011 so clearly demonstrates. The European Union and European civil society needs to engage in renewed dialogue with Islamic civil societies in the Middle East, based on mutual learning, respect and understanding. Such a dialogue is also required within Europe's borders, where Muslim groups are marginalized and excluded. Diasporic groups, especially those from North African countries, and Islamic religious leaders in Europe, provide a unique channel and a hitherto little used opportunity for the European Union to forge new partnerships with the emergent voices of Arab civil society.

Above all, this will demand a rethinking of European policy and its approach to the Israeli-Palestinian conflict. Although the EU supported and helped monitor the 2006 elections to the Palestinian Legislative Council, it has refused to engage with Hamas who emerged as the victorious party. The EU has been boycotting all contact with the Hamas-led Palestinian government in Gaza, as well as any official contact with Hamas, until Hamas accepts the three conditions laid out by the Quartet: 1) renunciation of violence; 2) recognition of Israel; and 3) acceptance of all previous agreements between Israel and the PLO. Instead the EU has channeled its financial and political support over the past five years to Palestinian President Mahmoud Abbas and the Palestinian Authority in the West Bank. Such an approach was seen by many in Europe as counterproductive, even prior to the Arab Spring.[11] As Michael Schulz argues, Europe's one-sided support for the corrupt Fatah-dominated Palestinian Authority has contributed to a weakening of democratization and human rights within Palestinian society.

The past year saw pressure from within Palestinian civil society for Hamas and Fatah to set aside their differences. This led to the signing on 4 May 2011 of the Reconciliation Agreement. Although the EU welcomed the move, it has done little beyond offering declaratory support to foster the conditions to enable the two sides to implement the terms of the agreement. Similarly, the Arab Spring will force the EU to rethink its donor assistance programs towards the Palestinians. In the past EU donor assistance has excluded Islamic charity organizations because they were considered part of Islamic political movements, even though those organizations have played an important role in encouraging democratization and offer support to the weakest sectors of Palestinian society.

The Arab Spring creates a number of challenges, both short- and long-term, for the European Union. Many of the authors in this volume argue that the European Union must now take the opportunity to learn from the lessons of the past and develop a new approach in its relations with the countries and societies of North Africa and the Middle East. Lorenzo Fioramonti presents the case for the development of a new paradigm for European foreign policy, a people based approach that offers a truer focus on human security. The European Union, with its past emphasis on security, stability and the protection of its borders and commercial interests, is seen by many in the region as part of the problem, not part of the solution. Fioramonti and Pace argue that Europe needs to step back and become a facilitator of democracy rather than promote its own conceptions of order and society. Middle Eastern societies are undergoing a process of reconstruction and are developing a new relationship and social contract between citizen(ship) and state based on fundamental freedoms, social rights, dignity and the rule of law. Europe must listen to the voices emerging from the region and enter into a dialogue with their definitions of freedom and democracy. It needs to engage in a process of self-reflection and learn from the past. It is the hope that this book, in some modest way, will contribute to that process.

Notes

1. European Commission, "Communication from the Commission to the Council on the Commission Proposals for Action Plans under the European Neighbourhood Policy (ENP)," COM(2004) 795 final. Brussels: December 9, 2004, 2.

2. Štephan Füle, "Speech on the recent events in North Africa," Speech/11/130. Brussels: February 28, 2011, 2. Accessed November 4, 2011, http://europa.eu/rapid/pressReleasesAction.do?reference=SPEECH/11/130.

3. European Commission, "Reinvigorating EU Actions on Human Rights and Democratisation with Mediterranean Partners—Strategic Guidelines," COM(2003) 294 final. Brussels: May 21, 2003, 13.

4. Štephan Füle, "Speech on the recent events in North Africa," Speech/11/130. Brussels: February 28, 2011, 2. Accessed November 4, 2011, http://europa.eu/rapid/pressReleasesAction.do?reference=SPEECH/11/130.

5. ENPI Information Centre, "EU and Tunisia Agree to Work Towards Advanced Status," May 11, 2010, accessed October 17, 2011, http://www.enpi-info.eu/mainmed.php?id_type=1&id=21537.

6. ENPI Information Centre, "EU and Tunisia Agree to Work towards Advanced Status." May 11, 2010, accessed October 17, 2011, http://www.enpi-info.eu/mainmed.php?id_type=1&id=21537.

7. "Remarks on Egypt and Tunisia," Catherine Ashton speech to the European Parliament, February 2, Speech/11/66, accessed November 7, 2001, http://www.isis-europe.org/pdf/2011_artrel_620_110325 libyastatements(1).pdf.

8. Council conclusions on Bahrain, 3091st Foreign Affairs Council meeting, Brussels, May 23, 2011. Accessed on November 4, 2011, http://www.consilium.europa.eu/uedocs/cms_Data/docs/.../122162.pdf.

9. European Commission, "A Partnership for Democracy and Shared Prosperity With the Southern Mediterranean," Brussels, March 8, 2011, COM(2011) 200 final.

10. European Commission, "A New Response to A Changing Neighbourhood: A Review of the European Neighbourhood Policy," Brussels, May 25, 2011, COM(2011) 303 final: 1.

11. See Clara O'Donnell, "The EU, Israel and Hamas," Center for European Reform Working Paper, 2008. Accessed on November 7, 2001, http://www.cer.org.uk/sites/default/files/publications/.../wp_820-1475.pdf

1

Reversing the Hierarchy of Priorities in EU-Mediterranean Relations

Jean-Pierre Cassarino

Respect for human rights and democratic principles has been regularly cited as an "essential element" of cooperation and relations between the European Union (EU) and non-EU countries in the Mediterranean. Since the 1990s onwards, numerous communications from the European Commission (EC) have stressed the need to integrate the so-called "essential-element" clause into the various agreements concluded with Mediterranean non-EU countries.

When concluding their association agreements with the European Union, Mediterranean countries agreed to respect the "essential-element" clause. When the European Neighborhood Policy (ENP) was introduced in 2004, the promotion of democracy and respect for human rights were presented as core values shaping the EU's external action in non-EU countries. ENP action plans, which were jointly agreed between the EU and each non-EU country, identified objectives seeking to "promote partners' commitment to common values such as the rule of law, good governance, respect for human rights, and the promotion of good neighborly relations."[1]

Moreover, a plethora of policy dialogues on human rights, at governmental and intergovernmental levels, have been regularly promoted with a view to "encouraging joint actions for democratization and human rights instruments." Pro-democracy programs were implemented and funded in the framework of the European Initiative for Democracy and Human Rights (EIDHR).

Despite the clear objectives mentioned in the ENP action plans, and the numerous dialogues designed to raise awareness of the need for democratic reforms and human rights, the promotion of democracy in Mediterranean non-EU countries has been, by all accounts, the least effective[2] chapter of Euro-Med cooperation. This lack of commitment has been denounced by various human rights organizations and associations. Likewise, the European Commission (EC) recognized on various occasions its failure in promoting the observance of human rights.

This chapter investigates how "essential" the human rights component has been compared with the diverse priorities contained in the European Neighborhood Policy (ENP). It sets out to demonstrate that a subtle hierarchy of priorities has shaped EU policy options and perceptions, making progress on human rights and democratization an issue of concern, but, at the same time, a dismissible priority in Euro-Mediterranean relations.

An Overall Set of Highly Heterogeneous Priorities

As early as the mid-1990s, the need to assess progress in the field of human rights observance, respect for the rule of law and political reforms became a key concern for the European Commission. Of course, criteria were necessary to understand the level of commitment to the rule of law of a given non-EU country in order to monitor progress and react accordingly.

However, the definition of such criteria, and respect therefore, was not a prerequisite to initiating negotiations with any given country. Rather, for an association agreement to be negotiated and concluded it sufficed that a formal commitment be made by the authorities of a non-EU country to (more) human rights observance and to (more) democracy. As stated in a communication of the European Commission, dated November 1995:

> The question is should we determine in advance the appraisal criteria, or is the very act of initiating negotiations with a country liable to have a beneficial impact on the way the situation develops? One condition does seem to be essential: the country concerned must make a clear commitment to the democratization process and undertake to respect the international principles and commitments to which it has subscribed.[3]

The rationale underpinning this approach was that regimes would have changed gradually through repeated interactions, incentives, and bilateral and multilateral dialogues. This rationale dismissed, or simply overlooked, the adaptive resilience of authoritarian regimes as well as their capacity for transformation and leverage. It also reflected the dominant vision that the European Union had the normative power to instill its own values and principles beyond its borders. This interpretation may explain why the need to subscribe to internationally recognized standards on human and civil rights was viewed as a first step towards possible regime change and democratic reforms in non-EU countries.

However, this assumption does not fully explain the lack of clear criteria aimed at assessing progress in the field of human rights observance. Stating that human rights and democratic principles constitute essential components of the EU external action does not say much about how essential these components are compared with other equally "essential," if not crucial, components of EU foreign policy. Nor does it imply that they constitute key drivers in the numerous assistance programs of the Commission, such as the MEDA program. Hence, we understand that setting clear appraisal criteria as applied to democratic reforms would have turned human rights observance into an end in itself, jeopardizing the neo-liberal orthodoxy that has shaped and driven Euro-med relations.

True, the promotion of human rights and democracy has always been part and parcel of an overall set of highly heterogeneous priorities. Moreover, human rights observance has been systematically included in the assistance programs of the EU. However, although this inclusion has been key to showing non-EU countries the fundamental values on which the Union is built and how it wishes to be perceived from the outside, these values have been far from being systematically shared by partners, despite the recurrence of regional political dialogues on human rights.

In its attempt to reinvigorate EU actions on human rights advocacy, the Commission itself starkly admitted in May 2003 that such dialogues with officials in Mediterranean non-EU countries did "not lead to a discussion of substance. On the contrary, [they] can serve as a pretext to avoid serious discussion [on the respect for human rights and democratic reforms in Mediterranean countries]."[4] This statement echoed previous (and recurrent) criticisms of those countries' capacity to engage in "a sufficiently frank and serious dialogue" and called for more effective initiatives to "promote respect for universal human rights."[5]

Against all logical expectations, such explicit self-criticism did not call for the definition of clear criteria aimed at assessing progress in the field of respect for human rights and democratic reforms.[6] The main reason is that, as explained above, setting clear criteria would have run counter to the predominant search for "stability, security and prosperity," which became the main pillars of the European Neighborhood Policy (ENP) that the EU adopted in 2003/2004 to reinvigorate its relations with Mediterranean non-EU countries.

Rhetoric and Practice

As a result of the enlargement of the EU, the ENP was introduced as a strategic response to neighboring countries in the East of Europe and in the South of the Mediterranean. It was also a direct EU response[7] to the controversial Greater Middle East (GME) initiative that the United States was concocting, under the Bush administration, before disclosing its rationale during the June 2004 G8 Summit in Sea Island. The US-led GME was met with strong skepticism among EU officials. As Tamara Cofman Wittes and Richard Youngs clearly explained, the European

Union suspected that "closer transatlantic cooperation on Middle Eastern reform," together with the "damaged reputation" of the United States in the Middle East region following the post-9/11 war on terror, would have jeopardized the influence and credibility of the EU, as well as its autonomy and image.[8] This is not the place to delve into these issues. Suffice it to say that both the ENP and the GME (today's Broader Middle East) are overlapping policy agendas competing for influence in the MENA region. At the same time, regardless of their respective *modus operandi* and the common rhetoric on democracy promotion in the region, both initiatives share the basic idea that democratic reforms should (at least in theory) be conditionally rewarded with liberal economic reforms, free market, special trade concessions, and enhanced development and financial aid. In practice however, "the correlation between reform and financial rewards has remained limited,"[9] leading to a resilient gap between pro-democracy rhetoric and practice.

Three factors contributed to gradually sidelining democratization and respect for human rights in Arab countries.

The first one relates to the empowerment of all North African countries following their proactive involvement in the reinforced control of the EU external borders and the fight against unauthorized migration in the Mediterranean. Cooperation has not only allowed these countries to play the efficiency card in migration talks. It has also allowed their strategic position to be capitalized upon while exerting a strong leverage on the EU and its Member States (particularly France, Italy, Spain, and the UK).[10] Reinforced cooperation on migration and border controls has since become an issue of high politics in Euro-Med relations. Linked to this, the drive for operability and flexibility has been prioritized by the EU and its Member States in their interaction with Mediterranean countries. This prioritization process has also contributed to weakening calls for democratic and human rights reforms. The most emblematic case is certainly the way in which the bilateral cooperation on the removal or readmission of unauthorized migrants has developed over the last ten years or so between the EU Member States and Mediterranean non-EU countries, particularly Libya and Tunisia. Cooperation has been intensified despite their lack of a well-functioning asylum system and their poor human rights record.

Secondly, there can be no question that the consolidation of a security paradigm has contributed to favoring the adoption of measures prioritizing the superior need to respond to perceived threats (e.g., Islamic fundamentalism, terrorism, migration and border controls) viewed as sources of instability. This was particularly so following the political landslide made by religious political parties through electoral processes in Egypt and the Occupied Palestinian Territories.

The third factor pertains to the predominant search for stability, an elusive notion *par excellence*. Both "political stability and democracy" were mentioned as one of the three main objectives[11] of the Euro-Mediterranean partnership. Some Mediterranean non-EU countries quickly reacted to the need for "political stability and democracy." For example, Tunisia, under the Ben Ali regime, skillfully reinterpreted this notion, with the support of the Tunisian official media, to portray itself as the epitome of stability and political openness (see chapter by Pinfari in this volume). Political stability has indeed been mixed in official rhetoric with "good governance," that is, the resilience of regimes, not regime change through fair and transparent electoral processes. Such notions as stability, good governance, economic liberalization, privatization, freedom to invest, and industrial restructuring have not only been part and parcel of the requirements contained in the neo-liberal agenda of association agreements. Such notions have also contributed to reifying the centrality of the state apparatus and of its authoritarian regime, paving the way for stronger state interference in the control of the economy and society. Tunisia is again a case in point. Not only did the Tunisian state and its presidential leadership portray themselves as the bulwark against religious fundamentalism, they also acted as the protectors against the challenges of globalization and as the superior pedagogues teaching society at large how to meet the liberal objectives of the association agreement with the EU.[12] Clearly, far from leading to state divestiture, the Tunisian state and its leadership skillfully buttressed their central position and control over the economy. Zealous private entrepreneurs who challenged the centrality of the state were defamed in the official press or urged to quit. Such coercive measures were emblematic of the threshold beyond which autonomous private initiatives could not prosper, in an open-door economic context, without the prior approval of the ruling party and the presidential leadership.[13]

Moreover, the Tunisian regime succeeded in conveying the idea that the success or failure of its partnership with the EU (which became the first Mediterranean country to have its association agreement ratified in March 1998) would determine the viability of other association agreements with additional non-EU countries in the Mediterranean region. This cause-and-effect relationship sounded like a threat to EU officials eager to turn a blind eye to the liberal *dirigisme* of the Tunisian regime (dubbed a model of economic miracle) and, consequently, to its illiberal social consequences.[14]

The foregoing is important to understand because when the ENP was launched in 2003–2004, notions of stability, prosperity, and security were already deep-rooted in the official propaganda of the EU's Mediterranean neighbors, of course with a different understanding and perception. This established context has had serious implications for the meaningfulness of the ENP conditionalities in the field of human rights, as well as their rationale. It also sheds light on how some policy options have been gradually prioritized over others, leading to the gradual consolidation of a hierarchy of priorities.

A Subtle Hierarchy of Priorities

I started this chapter by explaining that the sidelining of human rights concerns and political reforms in Mediterranean non-EU countries lies at the intersection of 1) the latter's empowerment in such strategic issues as the fight against unauthorized migration, border controls, and counterterrorism, 2) the consolidation of a security paradigm, and 3) the predominant search for stability.

It is the combination of the above three factors, not their individual impact, which has gradually shaped policy concerns and codified state-to-state relations in Euro-Mediterranean relations over the last fifteen years or so. Such relations have been codified as a result of the subtle consolidation of a hierarchy of priorities. A hierarchy of priorities could be defined as a set of policy priorities whose main function is to delineate the contours of the perceived top priorities that should be tackled first and foremost, while hiding others. Such "other" priorities are objectively as essential as other priorities. However, their relevance or criticality can hardly be translated in concrete terms, let alone be adequately considered, owing to their low position in the hierarchy. In other words, although they are objectively essential, they are not necessarily perceived as being so in practice. The subtlety of a hierarchy of priorities lies precisely in its capacity to show and hide at the same time. It is subtle insofar as it turns what was initially viewed as being essential into something that, eventually, is secondary or even dismissible.[15]

In the same vein, a hierarchy of priorities occurs through a process of consensus formation leading to the identification of top priorities and perceived exigencies. Consensus formation is, in turn, contingent on the repetition of shared principles and understandings upon which state-to-state cooperation is built. Obviously, repetition takes place through regular interactions or "dialogues" among state actors. It is precisely the repetition and periodicity of high-level policy meetings that contribute to instilling guiding principles and shared priorities in the minds of officials, decision-makers, the media, and the public. To rephrase Hannah Arendt, repetition is a key ingredient giving plausibility to (political) discourses, not because they are founded on true evidence, but because they are repeatedly presented as being so.[16]

The cooperation on deportation, reinforced border controls, and the fight against unauthorized migration are perhaps the most (though not the only) symptomatic features of this process of consensus formation. Today, these issues stand high in the hierarchy of priorities set by countries in the Euro-Mediterranean area, whether they be poor or rich, large or small, democratically organized or authoritarian.[17] It is indeed astonishing to observe that cooperation has developed regardless of whether all the countries in the Euro-Mediterranean area possess the capacity to fully respect the fundamental rights and the dignity of the expelled unauthorized migrants.

Likewise, a hierarchy of priorities filters our categories of thought and allows necessary evil to be accepted, if not justi-fied. It is under these circumstances, fraught with dominant subjectivities, apodictic statements, and stereotypes (e.g., "De-mocracy is incompatible with Arab cultures," "Arab nations are immune to democratization"), that violent repression against any kind of legitimate domestic opposition, whether organized or spontaneous, religious or secular, individual or collective was condemned. Before the Arab revolts, dissent was treated as a deviance, not as dissent. Genuine political opposition was viewed as a potential threat to "stability" by political regimes in Mediterranean non-EU countries, and their violent repression was too often met with silent acquiescence by European elites.

It is also under such circumstances that monitoring mecha-nisms aimed at assessing progress in the field of fundamental rights, democratization, and respect for human rights could not rank high in this hierarchy of priorities, nor could they acquire their real importance and policy relevance.

Reversing the Hierarchy of Priorities?

On 8 March 2011, the EU expressed its support for the radi-cal political transformations taking place in the Mediterranean neighborhood by proposing a "partnership for democracy and shared prosperity." The "new approach" implies a rethink of the ENP, based more proactively and unambiguously on economic and political reforms, democracy, and social justice. The new partnership document stated that "a radically changing politi-cal landscape in the Southern Mediterranean requires a change in the EU's approach to the region—the underlying themes of differentiation, conditionality and of a partnership between our societies are part of the ongoing review of the European Neigh-borhood Policy."[18]

Additionally, the EU stressed that a new partnership with lo-cal societies will be implemented with a view to reinforcing the role and advocacy capacity of civil society organizations (CSOs) and non-governmental organizations (NGOs) in the region. This would take place by facilitating their access to EU funds through the creation of a Civil Society Facility and through the establishment of the European Endowment for Democracy.[19] The strong emphasis placed in the current rethink of the ENP on the role of civil society is certainly reflective of the awareness that "Europe was not vocal enough in defending human rights and local democratic forces in the region,"[20] as Štephan Füle, the Commissioner responsible for enlargement and European Neighborhood Policy, recognized.

At the same time, however, such CSO-friendly initiatives may reflect the desire to regulate the claims of civil society actors through the establishment of managed (and manageable) channels of communication between government officials and CSOs, and through the selective allocations of EU funds. The haste with which such instruments have been put forward by EU officials, added to their strong emphasis on "synergies and coherence," calls for caution. Actually, given this emphasis, one is entitled to wonder whether the Civil Society Facility and the European Endowment for Democracy will establish new channels of communication with CSOs to critically address the pervasiveness of the above-mentioned hierarchy of priorities. This critical approach is by all means a prerequisite to establishing a genuine and meaningful exchange of ideas between CSOs, on the one hand, and states and international organizations, on the other, in all policy areas including the ways in which conditionalities as applied to the observance of human rights have been dealt with in the European Neighbourhood Policy (ENP).

Before the Arab revolts, two paradoxical factors explained the failure of the European Union to fully support civil society, or even to open regular channels of dialogue and consultations with them. On the one hand, officials in the EU and its Member States were perfectly aware that civil society organizations in many Arab countries were closely monitored by the state apparatus and the ruling party. For example, in Tunisia, law 92-25, dated April 1992, was enacted to control the activities and financial resources of associations through the strong interference of the ruling party. This legal instrument was clearly aimed at limiting the political clout of prominent civil society organizations in Tunisia, particularly the *Ligue Tunisienne des Droits de l'Homme*. On the other hand, given the pervasive control of the state apparatus on society, it is possible to assume that the EU and its Member States suspected any uncontrolled civil society actor as being potentially infiltrated or financially supported by Islamist movements. Both paradoxical factors might have shaped the perceptions as well as the political willingness of the EU and its Member States to deal with CSOs in Arab countries, to understand their rationale and listen to their claims. Moreover, both factors may reflect the awareness among most government officials in the EU that opening channels of communication with local CSOs, whether infiltrated or not, would have become ineffective in political terms, if not counterproductive with regard to the predominant search for "stability."

Today, the rethink of the ENP will depend on how conditionalities will genuinely integrate and reflect the *primacy* of human rights, respect for individual freedoms and social justice. More importantly, this primacy will be contingent on the need to reverse the hierarchy of priorities that has so far determined policy options and justified, by the same token, the resilience of a security paradigm in Euro-Mediterranean relations.

Meeting this challenge is by no means easy. Despite its expressed sense of guilt and clear desire to learn from past errors, and despite its intention to open dialogue with societies and not only with political elites in the South, the EU will continue to respond to the diverging short-term policy interests of its twenty-seven Member States, particularly in terms of foreign policy in the Mediterranean, economic cooperation and business alliances, energy security, border controls, and migration management issues.

Towards "New Subjectivities"

Has the possibility of reversing the hierarchy of priorities become hopeless given that we are confronted with powerful paradigms that continue to shape policy options and categories of thought with reference to the Southern Mediterranean?

To reply to this question, it is necessary to stress that the social movements spreading through the Southern Mediterranean since December 2010 have led to protests that were not the direct or indirect off-shoots of EU financial assistance to civil societies,[21] for example, under the EIDHR. Rather, they have taken place well outside its remit, confounding the stability logic that has long driven policy options in Euro-Mediterranean relations.

It is equally important to emphasize that, as a result of growing social and political protests, Arab regimes have been faced, to varying degrees, with unprecedented demands for public accountability that they can no longer ignore. Today, their citizens are well aware that freedom of expression is more than a value to be treasured; it determines the contours of a changing relationship between themselves and their governments and may contribute to shaping the upcoming social and political developments in their countries. The vibrant civil and political bodies that have emerged since early 2011 have to be factored by Arab governments into their policies, for the sake of their own survival and domestic legitimacy.

True, CSOs today have a critical role to play in heading towards new forms of democratic control. True also, to overcome subordination to power in its various forms, independent thinking will be necessary to gradually reverse the hierarchy of priorities mentioned above. Credible information and counter-knowledge are key elements to achieving this. However, in absolute terms, neither element would suffice to turn CSO involvement into decisive policy change in the Southern Mediterranean. Actually, the capacity of CSOs to think out of the box will remain contingent on their capacity to acquire an authoritative role and to provide real alternatives that may cast doubt on dominant schemes of interpretation. Against this backdrop, the participation of CSOs in EU-sponsored dialogues and initiatives, through the Civil Society Facility, might hardly be conducive to expressions of "new subjectivities," as Foucault would put it, indispensable to empower local CSOs. Democrats and civil society actors in Arab countries would be well-advised to rely on their own resources. Their emancipation will not depend *only* on more financial support, let alone on channels of interaction established from the top.

Rather, their emancipation will depend on their ability to create and structure their *own* channels of communication with decision-makers and the population at large, and above all, out of the realm of states' interference. This is the biggest challenge they are currently confronted with. Such channels have to be organized through collective action, not individually, insofar as the coalition of like-minded civil society organizations is the only way of creating the right conditions by which to interact with decision-makers on an equal basis. Such collective action is possible now that thinking differently can no longer be dubbed a form of deviance or viewed by the West as a threat to "stability." It is time to realize that, with or without the financial assistance of the EU to CSOs in Arab countries, the current historical context is ripe to create the preconditions needed to question the hierarchy of priorities and to undo its constructs.

Notes

The author is grateful to Raffaella Del Sarto for comments on an earlier draft.

1. European Commission, "Communication from the Commission to the Council on the Commission Proposals for Action Plans under the European Neighbourhood Policy (ENP)," COM(2004) 795 final. Brussels: December 9, 2004, 2.

2. If we consider that "effective" refers to the extent to which the EU and its Member States have exerted their own leverage to press for (more) human rights observance and respect for fundamental freedoms. Arguably, this point remains questionable if we consider the poor EU financial resources earmarked for human rights programs and activities in the Mediterranean; see Federica Bicchi, Laura Guazzone, Daniela Pioppi, eds., *La questione della democrazia nel mondo arabo: stati, società e conflitti.* (Monza: Polimetrica, 2004).

3. European Commission, "The European Union and the External Dimension of Human Rights Policy: From Rome to Maastricht and Beyond," COM/95/567 final. Brussels: November 22, 1995, 22.

4. European Commission, "Reinvigorating EU Actions on Human Rights and Democratisation with Mediterranean Partners—Strategic Guidelines," COM(2003) 294 final. Brussels: May 21, 2003, 13.

5. European Commission, "Reinvigorating the Barcelona Process," COM(2000) 297 final. Brussels: October 6, 2000, 4.

6. On benchmarking democratic progress, see Raffaella Del Sarto, Tobias Schumacher, Erwan Lannon with Ahmed Driss "Benchmarking Democratic Development in the Euro-Mediterranean Area: Conceptualising Ends, Means and Strategies," *EuroMeSCOAnnual Report 2006.* (Lisbon: EUROMESCO, 2007).

7. Rosemary Hollis, "The UfM and the Middle East 'Peace Process': An Unhappy Symbiosis," *Mediterranean Politics* 16, no. 1 (2011): 106.

8. Tamara Cofman Wittes and Richard Youngs, "Europe, the United States, and Middle Eastern Democracy: Repairing the Breach," *The Saban Center for Middle East Policy, Brookings Institution, Analysis Paper* no. 18, (2009): 3–5.

9. Cofman Wittes and Youngs, "Europe, the United States," 9.

10. Jean-Pierre Cassarino, ed., *Unbalanced Reciprocities: Cooperation on Readmission in the Euro-Mediterranean Area* (Washington D.C.: The Middle East Institute, 2010), 16–18.

11. The three objectives included: 1) strengthening political stability and democracy in a common area of peace and security; 2) creating an area of shared economic prosperity and supporting the creation of a free trade area between the EU and its Mediterranean partners by 2010; and 3) establishing closer links between the peoples of these countries through cultural, social, and human partnerships.

12. Jean-Pierre Cassarino, "The EU-Tunisian Association Agreement and Tunisia's Structural Reform Program," *Middle East Journal* 53, no. 1 (1999): 60. See also, Emma C. Murphy, "The Tunisian *Mise à Niveau* Programme and the Political Economy of Reform," *New Political Economy* 11, no. 4 (2006): 519–40.

13. Cassarino, "The EU-Tunisian Association Agreement," 69–71.

14. See Béatrice Hibou, *La Force de l'obéissance: Economie politique de la répression en Tunisie* (Paris: La Découverte, 2006).

15. For an in-depth reflection on how policy priorities and choices are ordered and re-ordered over time, see the essay of French philosopher Vladimir Jankélévitch, *Le Je-ne-sais-quoi et le Presque-rien: La méconnaissance, le malentendu* (Paris: Editions du Seuil, 1980), 36–38.

16. Hannah Arendt, *Edifier un monde: Interventions 1971–1975,* trans. Mira Koller and Dominique Séglard (Paris: Editions du Seuil, 2007). The most worrying aspect, for Hannah Arendt, lies in that

those who give and receive the plausible "truth" may play interchangeable roles.

17. Cassarino, *Unbalanced Reciprocities*, 21.

18. European Commission, "A Partnership for Democracy and Shared Prosperity with the Southern Mediterranean," COM(2011) 200 final. Brussels, March 8, 2011, 3.

19. European Commission and High Representative, "A New Response to a Changing Neighbourhood," COM(2011) 303 final. Brussels: May 25, 2011, 4.

20. Štephan Füle, "Speech on the recent events in North Africa," Speech/11/130. Brussels: February 28, 2011, 2. Accessed November 4, 2011, http://europa.eu/rapid/pressReleasesAction.do?reference=SPEECH/11/130.

21. Benoît Challand, "The Arab Revolts and the Cage of Political Economy," *Insurgent Notes: Journal Of Communist Theory and Practise*, no. 4 (2011): 134.

2

Promoting Human Rights and Democracy

A New Paradigm for the European Union

Lorenzo Fioramonti

The founding principles of the European Union (EU) derive, among other sources, from the 1948 Universal Declaration of Human Rights and the following 1966 UN Covenants on Civil, Political and Economic Rights. Moreover, human rights and democracy are at the core of the European integration process (which was built over the ashes of civil war and genocide) and its long-term aspirations. Invariably, therefore, the recognition of human rights and democracy reverberates in the EU's foreign policy and external relations. Yet, the performance of the EU as an active promoter of human rights and democracy has been marked by inconsistencies and double standards, against the backdrop of a general process of "securitization," that is, a tendency to prioritize international and internal security. Needless to say, this has often led to an inversion of priorities in the external policies towards some regions of the world, chiefly North Africa and the Middle East (but also, though to a lesser degree, in Eurasia), where the EU has entertained rather cozy relations with autocrats and dictators as a means to guarantee a rather narrowly defined notion of "stability."

The seemingly unstoppable wave of revolutions in North Africa and the Middle East challenges this approach not only from a moral perspective, but also from an empirical viewpoint.

Most of these regimes turned out to be less resilient than assumed. They literally crumbled under the growing pressure of social movements and opposition forces. Rather than acting as buffers against the potential upsurge of Islamist political parties (traditionally considered the worse evil by the EU and its Member States), these authoritarian governments inflicted decades of hardship, abuse and repression on their own populations, thereby strengthening religiously inspired opposition forces and so-called political Islam. In turn, this damaged the image of Europe in the eyes of local populations, who largely viewed the EU and its Member States as complicit with their oppressors.

Building on events of the Arab Spring and its impact on the credibility of Europe as a genuine partner, this chapter calls for a fundamental overhaul of the EU's approach to the promotion of human rights and democracy, taking into consideration the centrality of individuals as actors in the international arena. By drawing on the EU's focus on "human security" centered on the "people first" principle, I argue that a new paradigm for the promotion of human rights and democracy should be based on the primacy of individuals, including their basic needs, their aspirations and their freedom to govern themselves in whatever way they prefer. By developing the capacity to "listen," the EU should shift its role from "promoter" to that of "facilitator" of democracy. In order to unpack this argument, the next section looks at the EU's traditional policies for the promotion of human rights and democracy, while the central section focuses on human security and describes how its key tenets should inspire a fundamental revision of the EU's approach.

The Inconsistencies of the EU's Promotion of Human Rights and Democracy

Human rights and democracy are at the core of the European integration process and its long-term aspirations. All member states are constitutional democracies and share a set of common values based on civil, political and social rights. Article 6 of the consolidated version of the Treaty on the European Union (TEU) establishes the founding values of the EU:

> The European Union is founded on the principles of liberty, democracy, respect for human rights and fundamental freedoms, and the rule of law, principles which are common to the Member States.[1]

Moreover, Article 7 introduces institutional mechanisms to punish serious and persistent violations of human rights and democracy by Member States, a provision that was further strengthened by the modifications introduced in 2000 by the Treaty of Nice.

Human rights and democracy are also the cornerstones of the so-called Copenhagen criteria, which govern the accession process of EU candidate countries. Building on Article 49 of the Treaty on the European Union, which establishes that any country seeking membership must conform to the EU's fundamental values, the Copenhagen European Council in 1993 (and, in 1995, the Madrid European Council) also established that, for the EU to take into consideration a potential member, the candidate country must possess stable institutions guaranteeing, among others, the protection and promotion of human rights and democracy.

Invariably, the foundational recognition of human rights and democracy also reverberates in the EU's external relations, where they have become crosscutting elements permeating all economic relations, trade agreements and special partnerships with other countries.[2] In establishing the Common Foreign and Security Policy (CFSP), Article 11 of the Treaty on the European Union underlined that one of the Union's foreign policy goals was "respect for human rights and fundamental freedoms." Consequently, the objective of promoting human rights and democracy has also been extended to development policies and all other forms of cooperation with third countries in accordance with Article 177 of the consolidated version of the Treaty establishing the European Community (TEC), which affirms that EU development policy "shall contribute to the general objective of

[. . .] respecting human rights and fundamental freedoms."[3] This commitment was further strengthened in 2000 through the adoption of the EU Charter of Fundamental Rights, which enshrined the basic freedoms and rights of all European citizens and, ever since, it has also been guiding the EU's external promotion policies.

According to the 2001 Commission's communication on *The European Union's Role in Promoting Human Rights and Democracy in Third Countries*, the EU is well placed in the protection of human rights and democracy at the international level:

> Uniquely amongst international actors, all fifteen Member States of the Union are democracies espousing the same Treaty-based principles in their internal and external policies. This gives the EU substantial political and moral weight. Furthermore, as an economic and political player with global diplomatic reach, and with a substantial budget for external assistance, the EU has both influence and leverage, which it can deploy on behalf of democratisation and human rights.[4]

The promotion of human rights and democracy has always cut across the classical division of institutional authority. Some policies, such as sanctions, embargoes and military operations are decided upon and coordinated through an intergovernmental decision-making process, which is specific of both the Common Foreign and Security Policy and the European Security and Defence Policy. By contrast, all pro-democracy policies that necessitate direct assistance, political aid and cooperation are managed directly by the European Commission, generally through its cooperation office EuropeAid.[5] Political conditionality, that is, the inclusion of a number of clauses for the respect of human rights and democracy in the trade and partnership agreements signed with third countries, is the connecting element between communitarian policies (e.g., development aid) and intergovernmental decisions (e.g., sanctions). When these conditions are not respected (for instance, human rights and democracy are abused in a partner country), the EU can unilaterally decide to close the tap of development aid, suspend trade relations and even impose sanctions and embargoes. Moreover, since 1992, the

EU's practice has been to include a number of clauses concerning "essential elements" in all agreements with third countries with a view to also promoting the ratification of international human rights and democracy conventions and, through an institutionalized procedure of political dialogue, preventing the escalation of political crises.

Practically, the EU's approach to human rights and democracy in external relations can be divided into two areas: mainstreaming and direct promotion. The "mainstreaming" principle requires integrating human rights and democracy issues into all aspects of EU policy decision-making and implementation of external relations policies. In its relations with other countries, the EU defines detailed country strategy papers in which an assessment of the situation of human rights and democracy is included. This assessment is in turn an integral element of the assistance strategies adopted, with regular reviews providing the opportunity for expanding and refining references to human rights and democracy. Moreover, regional cooperation programs are also used to advance human rights and democracy cooperation. The main policy for direct promotion is the European Instrument for Democracy and Human Rights (EIDHR), adopted by the Council and the European Parliament in 2006 (previously known as "initiative"). It is supported by a special budget (of approximately €1 billion for the financial period 2007–2013) managed directly by the European Commission and works mainly through cooperation with civil society organizations, but also in partnership with some key international institutions. Furthermore, since 1995, the EU inserts a standard clause in all cooperation agreements with third countries, stating that respect for human rights and democracy constitutes an essential element of the agreement. Under this clause, sanctions may be put in place in response to serious violations of human rights and democracy. However, as argued by the EU, the principal role of the clause is to provide the Union with a basis for positive engagement on human rights and democracy issues with third countries. The Cotonou Agreement with the African, Caribbean, and Pacific (ACP) countries includes the latest version of the "essential elements" clause. It provides for consultations and dialogue with signatory countries where there have been violations so that human rights and democracy can be restored as quickly as possible. Finally, human rights and democracy are regularly addressed in the political dialogues that the EU conducts with third countries and regional groups. The aim is to gather information about the human rights and democracy situation in the country in question, or to express concern about the country's human rights and democracy record and identify practical steps to improve it.

As a matter of fact, the EU has often demonstrated hostility towards the use of heavy measures, such as sanctions and embargoes, for the external promotion of human rights and democracy. More generally it has favored a gradual approach characterized by political dialogue, development cooperation and democracy assistance, which is based on the conviction that rewarding positive attitudes towards political reform is a better long-term strategy than overtly punishing temporary setbacks.[6] This "carrot more than stick" approach has been utilized in many different circumstances, especially towards important trade partners, and was epitomized by the enlargement processes of 2004 and 2007, when nations from the former socialist bloc succeeded in joining the European "club" not always for tangible political and institutional merits. As part of this "soft" strategy to promote human rights and democracy, the EU has placed a significant emphasis on support for civil society.[7] At least in rhetorical terms, the EU has traditionally attributed a central role to civil society both in challenging authoritarian governments and in building/consolidating democracy: it is viewed as the most promising vehicle of incremental liberalization at the dawn of democracy and, during democratic consolidation, it is viewed as the best placed actor to rein in potentially dominant executives and encourage public participation.[8]

Assessing practice against the rhetoric, a number of observers have pointed to inconsistencies and double standards in the EU's actual policies for the promotion of human rights and democracy, including its alleged focus on supporting civil society.[9] On a number of occasions, the widely heralded goal of protecting and promoting human rights and democracy has been sidelined due to other (more compelling) interests, such as economic advantages, commercial gains and regional stability. Through a general process of "securitization," conventional fields of low politics, such as trade, investment and energy policies have been re-interpreted as security issues.[10] Thus, for instance, in order to guarantee energy security, the EU and its Member States have refrained from questioning the growing abuse of human rights and manipulation of democratic processes in the Eurasian region (particularly Russia and some of the Caucasian states). Similarly, for the sake of bilateral trade, the EU has also softened its condemnation of human rights abuses in China. Not surprisingly, the EU has traditionally shown a greater zeal in resorting to punitive measures for violations of human rights and democracy in those regions of the world where it had "the upper hand," particularly in the "poor, marginal countries" of sub-Saharan Africa.

In a recent discussion of Europe's policies towards North Africa and the Middle East after 2001, Jean Pierre Cassarino and Nathalie Tocci have argued that the EU's promotion of human rights and democracy in the southern Mediterranean has been guided by the fear that through open democratic processes Islamist parties would hold sway over national elections and ultimately take power.[11] As of 2005, this possibility had already become a reality: the Muslim Brotherhood won 88 out of 454 seats in the Egyptian parliamentary elections of 2005, before being outlawed by Mubarak's regime. Hizbollah enjoyed significant support in Lebanon's 2005 elections and then joined the coalition government; Hamas outpaced Fatah in the 2006 legislative elections in the Palestinian Territories, before being ostracized by the EU and the United States, which accused the political movement of being a terrorist organization.

Such an overarching fear of a political radicalization of the region led to a general shift in the European agenda, preferring the "stability" guaranteed by "friendly" dictators at the expense of the legitimate demands of the people. This process resulted in a compartmentalization of interregional relations, especially under the so-called Union for the Mediterranean, whereby European countries promoted commercial cooperation between the two shores of the *mare nostrum* (especially in the field of energy, transport and infrastructure) without questioning the political context in which such cooperation was embedded. Furthermore, in the field of migration control and management, the sustained cooperation between European countries and their southern Mediterranean counterparts gave the latter strategic leverage in migration and border management talks, weakening the EU's capacity to exert credible pressure on "democratization and human rights observance."[12] This general approach to human rights and democracy in North Africa and the Middle East reflects what Cassarino calls a "hierarchy of priorities" whereby pursuing effective interregional partnerships in a variety of strategic fields took precedence over fundamental questions regarding human rights and democracy.[13]

In spite of its proclaimed emphasis on the democratizing role of civil society, the EU has often superimposed its own notion of civil society (largely forged on the example of Western non-governmental organizations) on the real-life diversity of other countries' social movements and groups. In most regions of the world, this has led to a rather narrow focus on elite-based liberally minded civic organizations, as opposed to the wide variety of grassroots popular movements. In the case of North Africa and the Middle East, this bias was particularly evident: the vast majority of non-state actors, especially religiously inspired mass movements, were considered illegitimate by the EU (often because they were considered connected with Islamic parties) and were therefore excluded from any form of institutional dialogue, let alone financial support schemes. By refusing to engage with such a diverse universe of civil societies, the EU invariably lost touch with the "real people" and failed to capture the public mood that eventually culminated in the 2011 revolts. Indirectly, this type of relationship strengthened the region's autocrats, weakened genuine democratic processes and exasperated local populations.

A New Paradigm: A "People-based" Approach

Since the creation of the EU, the main objectives of the CFSP as detailed in article 11 of the Maastricht Treaty on the European

Union (TEU) were to "safeguard the [. . .] independence and integrity of the Union" while also helping "develop and consolidate democracy and the rule of law, and respect for human rights and international freedoms."[14] The 2003 European Security Strategy (ESS) underlined that "the post Cold War environment is one of increasingly open borders in which the internal and external aspects of security are indissolubly linked." It also pointed out the fundamental interconnectedness of security, human rights and democracy given that "a number of countries and regions are caught in a cycle of conflict, insecurity and poverty." In spite of its merits, the ESS focused primarily on systemic security, that is, the security of states and institutions, and did not see the breach of human rights *per se* as a security threat. It thus considered the protection of human rights and democracy a fundamental ingredient of a peaceful and secure international order:

> The best protection for our security is a world of well-governed democratic states. Spreading good governance, supporting social and political reforms, dealing with corruption and abuse of power, establishing the rule of law and protecting human rights are the best means of strengthening the international order.[15]

The 2003 ESS was followed in 2004 by the publication of the Barcelona Report of the Study Group on Europe's Security Capabilities, which developed what was then branded "a human security doctrine for Europe." The report concentrates on the principles that should guide the EU's direct intervention in cases of human rights violations perpetrated in other countries and puts forward a coherent strategic view, essentially focused on the "primacy of human rights." The adoption of this principle not only implies a fundamental respect for human rights during peace-keeping operations but also, and most importantly, it emphasizes that the defense and protection of individuals must be given primacy over efforts aimed at securing a "temporary suppression of violence."[16] Therefore, the Barcelona Report calls for a paradigmatic shift: policies and interventions have to be designed in order to protect and promote the rights of individuals, regardless whether this will lead to stability and security at the systemic level. In other words, the ultimate goal of EU policy and intervention should not be the pursuit of international security, but rather the protection of the basic needs and aspirations of the people.

Simply put, human security debunks the question of "security" from its traditional conception of the safety of states (or institutions) to the safety of people and communities. Moreover, once the reference object of security is changed to individuals, it then proposes to extend the notion of "safety" to a condition beyond mere existence (survival) to life worth living, hence, wellbeing and dignity of human beings. Thus, authoritarian rule, endemic poverty and human rights abuse, for example, are conceptualized as human security threats—not because they can induce violence and thus threaten the stability of the international system, but because they are antithetical to the dignity of individuals. In giving center stage to the safety of individuals, human security has undergone a conceptual shift from the notion of "threat" as implying imminent and tangible risk to the individual, to "vulnerability," which underlines the relationship between a condition of social, political and economic destitution and the ability of individuals to fulfill their aspirations.[17] This concept of human security is clearly influenced by Amartya Sen's reflections on human development as building individual capabilities and freedom (e.g., through education, social support and healthcare) rather than achieving systemic outcomes (e.g., growth in national income).[18]

In 2008, with the *Report on the Implementation of the European Security Strategy*, the EU partially revisited its approach to incorporate certain elements of the human security doctrine:

> We have worked to build human security, by reducing poverty and inequality, promoting good governance and human rights, assisting development, and addressing the root causes of conflict and insecurity. [. . .] We need to continue mainstreaming human rights issues in all activities in this field [. . .], through a people-based approach coherent with the concept of human security.[19]

The events of the 2011 Arab Spring and their consequences for EU strategy in the region clearly reveal that a "people-based approach" was far from coherently applied. Among other things, the systematic and consistent application of this approach should have led to a dialogue with the wide array of civil society expressions in North Africa and the Middle East, regardless of their political, social and cultural hue.

In the post Arab Spring world, a coherent application of a people-based approach holds the potential to reaffirm the EU's credibility in international affairs as a genuine defender of human rights and democracy. The key features of this new paradigm are presented in Table 2.1, along with an explanation of how they apply to the specific fields of human rights and democracy.

First of all, this approach would compel the EU to put human rights "first," regardless of the political and economic repercussions this might have on short-term strategic interests. This would also imply a holistic approach to human security, taking into consideration not only direct threats to human rights, but also the consequences that certain EU policies may have on the wellbeing and sustainable development of other countries. Needless to say, such a step would require a significant revision

Table 2.1. A People-based Approach to Human Rights and Democracy

Key Features of the people-based approach	Human Rights	Democracy
People first	Primacy of human rights	Non-prescriptive approach to democracy building
Holistic approach	Assessing impact that *all* European policies (e.g. trade, energy, security, migration) have on civil, political, cultural and economic rights	Assessing impact that *all* European policies (e.g. trade, energy, security, migration) have on democratic accountability and sustainable development
Civil society focus	Preference for civilian interposition forces in cases of human rights violations	Open dialogue with all civil society forces, favoring diversity
Facilitation	Support initiatives led by domestic groups	Support domestically driven institution building

of the Union's policies in a number of fields, including trade, energy and migration, which are likely to have a dramatic impact on the social, cultural and economic rights of non-European populations.

Moreover, a people-based approach would require the EU to shift from being a "promoter of democracy" to becoming a "facilitator of democratization," with two fundamental consequences. Firstly, it would mean adopting a non-prescriptive attitude: democracy can take many forms, some of which may be very different from the institutional experience of Europe and the Western world. There are no models, easy fixes or successful recipes for democratization, which remains a domestically driven process. In the same vein, there are no cultural characteristics or religious preconditions that inhibit or facilitate democracy. At the end of the day, the EU itself is a variegated composite of institutional forms, from parliamentary democracies to constitutional monarchies, with different degrees of influence exercised by religious groups, churches and sectarian movements. Secondly, the EU would need to realize that, while the extent to which external actors can support the process of democracy building is relatively limited, they are often more successful at undermining it. For instance, Western governments have a long tradition of meddling (both directly and indirectly) in the policies and decisions of other countries. In addition, European corporations have often conducted their businesses in ways that harmed human rights and democratic processes in other countries. This tendency becomes utterly unacceptable in the context of a people-based human rights and democracy strategy and would require monitoring and sanctioning instruments.

Finally, a people-based approach would require the EU to take civil society seriously, in all its forms and manifestations. Human beings are free to choose different ways to express their interests and values. Some may be more in line with the "taste" of the EU, while others may be less palatable. In spite of the inevitable difficulty of bridging cultural and religious divides, the people-centered approach demands a genuine commitment to openness and builds on a deep acceptance and understanding of the "other."

Conclusion

The strategies of the EU and its member states have for too long been guided by a hierarchy of priorities that put a narrowly conceived notion of "stability" at the top and which sideline a genuine commitment to human rights and democracy. The revolutions in North Africa and the Middle East demonstrated that far from being stable guarantors of order, these regimes were in fact themselves the cause of popular discontent and unrest.

Against this backdrop, this chapter calls for a paradigm shift in the way in which the EU formulates and implements its human rights and democracy promotion policies. By building on the concept of human security, largely debated within European institutions and intellectual circles, the chapter has discussed the potential of a coherent "people-based approach" to reaffirm the credibility of the EU as a genuine defender of human rights and a facilitator of democracy. In order to achieve this objective, not only the EU but also the whole of Europe will need to acknowledge past mistakes, shortcomings and vested interests, which have ultimately led to inconsistencies and double standards.

Besides its indirect acceptance of abuses and oppression within its own "neighborhood" and its inability to predict the chain of revolts in the Arab world, the EU's image in the eyes of many other countries has been weakened by the global financial crisis, which threatens to tear European integration apart. Millions of citizens in Europe are questioning the accountability of European institutions and demanding fundamental changes. The time has come for the EU to "listen," both abroad and at home, if it intends to reaffirm its credibility as a progressive institutional actor.

Notes

1. "Consolidated Versions of the Treaty on the European Union and of the Treaty Establishing the European Community," C321, 29 December 2006, accessed on October 15, 2011, http://eur-lex.europa.eu/LexUriServ/LexUriServ.do?uri=OJ:C:2006:321E:0001:0331:EN:PDF.

2. Sonia Lucarelli and Ian Manners, eds., *Values and Principles in European Union Foreign Policy* (London and New York: Routledge, 2006).

3. "Consolidated Versions of the Treaty on the European Union," 126.

4. "The European Union's Role in Promoting Human Rights and Democratisation in Third Countries," COM (2001) 252 final, accessed on October 15, 2011, http://eur-lex.europa.eu/smartapi/cgi/sga_doc?smartapi!celexplus!prod!DocNumber&lg=en&type_doc=COMfinal&an_doc=2001&nu_doc=252.

5. All member states have their own political aid strategies and funds: although invited to join the Commission's initiatives on the ground, Member States' policies have not always respected the general guidelines agreed upon in Brussels. Moreover, Member States run different and sometimes competitive policies, privileging specific aspects of development co-operation in accordance with contextual strategic goals.

6. Gordon Crawford, *Foreign Aid and Political Reform: A Comparative Analysis of Democracy Assistance and Political Conditionality* (Basingstoke: Palgrave, 2001).

7. Lorenzo Fioramonti, *European Union Democracy Aid: Supporting Civil Society in Post-Apartheid South Africa* (London: Routledge, 2010).

8. Richard Youngs, "Democracy Promotion: The Case of the European Union Strategy." *CEPS Working Document*, No.167 (2001).

9. Karen E. Smith, "The Use of Political Conditionality in the EU's Relations with Third Countries: How Effective?" *European Foreign Affairs Review* 3 no. 2 (1998): 253–74. See also A. Ward, "Frameworks for Cooperation between the EU and Third Countries: A Viable Matrix for Uniform Human Rights Standards," *European Foreign Affairs Review* 3 no. 3 (2001): 505–36.

10. For an overview of such a "securitization" process and its scale, please refer to the various papers and case studies recently published on the website of the project "EU-GRASP: The EU as a Global and Regional Actor in Security and Peace," accessed on October 15, 2011, http://www.eu-grasp.eu.

11. Jean-Pierre Cassarino and Nathalie Tocci, "The EU's Mediterranean policies after the Arab revolts: from crisis to a new order?" in *Regions and Crises: Challenges for Contemporary Regionalisms*, ed. Lorenzo Fioramonti (Basingstoke: Palgrave, forthcoming).

12. George Joffé, "The European Union, Democracy and Counter-Terrorism in the Maghreb," *Journal of Common Market Studies* 46 no. 1 (2008): 166.

13. Jean-Pierre Cassarino, ed., *Unbalanced Reciprocities: Cooperation on Readmission in the Euro-Mediterranean Area* (Washington, D.C.: The Middle East Institute, 2010), 21.

14. Treaty on the European Union, Title V, Article 11, accessed on October 15, 2011, http://www.consilium.europa.eu/uedocs/cmsUpload/treatychap5.pdf.

15. European Security Strategy, "A Secure Europe in a Better World," accessed on October 15, 2011, http://www.consilium.europa .eu/uedocs/cmsUpload/78367.pdf.

16. Mary Kaldor et al., "A Human Security Doctrine for Europe. The Barcelona Report of the Study Group on Europe's Security Capabilities," 2004, accessed November 4, 2011, http://www .globalgovernancewatch.org/resources/a-human-security-doctrine -for-europe—the-barcelona-report-of-the-study-group-on-europes -security-capabilities

17. Shahrbanou Tadjbakhsh and Anuradha M. Chenoy, *Human Security. Concepts and Implications* (London and New York: Routledge, 2009), 10. See also Mary Kaldor, *Human Security: Reflections on Globalization* (Cambridge: Polity Press, 2007).

18. Amartya Sen, *Development as Freedom* (Oxford: Oxford University Press, 2000). In 2003, when the former UN Secretary General Kofi Annan constituted a Commission on Human Security to reflect on the possibility to incorporate human security into the institutional setup of current global governance mechanisms, he invited Amartya Sen to take part in it.

19. Report on the Implementation of the European Security Strategy - Providing Security in a Changing World, Brussels, December 11, 2008 S407/08, accessed October 15, 2011, http://www.consilium.europa .eu/uedocs/NewsWord/en/esdp/104631.doc.

Baker College of Clinton Twp Library

3

Tunisia and Libya

Marco Pinfari

The Tunisian or "Jasmine" revolution and the Libyan civil war are two key episodes in the so-called Arab Spring. The Tunisian revolution was the first spark that indirectly ignited further revolts across the region, while the Libyan civil war is, at the time of writing (October 2011), the only episode in the Arab Spring that experienced substantial intervention by external actors.

The presence of tight economic and diplomatic links between North African countries and European countries and the European Union (EU) as an institution created widespread expectations that the EU would play a substantial role in helping the democratic transitions in North Africa as mandated by article 21 of the Lisbon Treaty, according to which:

> The Union's action on the international scene shall be guided by the principles which have inspired its own creation, development and enlargement, and which it seeks to advance in the wider world: democracy, the rule of law, the universality and indivisibility of human rights and fundamental freedoms.[1]

This general framework, however, clashed with some hard facts. For instance, in 1995 the EU had signed an Association Agreement with Tunisia and had close diplomatic and political relations with the country by the time the revolution began; no such agreement, however, exists with Libya, even if preliminary negotiations have been underway since 2008. Most importantly, at the political and diplomatic level, bilateral relations between European and North African countries, often informed by pre-existing colonial links, have developed into a complex network of interests far more intricate than the cooperation frameworks negotiated by the EU Commission.

Both episodes thus call for a broad assessment of the ways in which key political, economic and diplomatic interests and values were articulated by European actors to shape their responses to these crises. In this regard two key questions seem particularly relevant. The main question in relation to the Tunisian case is arguably whether, and how effectively, the EU used its extensive political and diplomatic bonds with Ben Ali's regime to help the democratic transition of the country before, during and immediately after the revolution. In the Libyan civil war, it is instead interesting to assess how the EU reacted to the opportunity to act as "policeman" in its neighborhood, and to exercise political and (possibly) military leadership in addressing what was broadly perceived as a humanitarian crisis nested into the outset of a democratic transition.

Tunisia and the Case for Democratic Conditionality

The Jasmine revolution began on 17 December 2010 following the act of self-immolation of Mohammed Buazizi, a fruit and vegetable seller who set himself on fire on 17 December 2010 after his cart was confiscated by police. In the following weeks demonstrations led to a number of clashes with police forces, most notably on 24–27 December 2010, and were accompanied by a number of strikes and acts of civil resistance. The crisis further escalated on 8–12 January 2011 with another series of violent encounters between police forces and demonstrators, which was followed on 14 January by the decision by Tunisian President Zine El Abdine Ben Ali to impose a state of emergency and fire his cabinet. Later that day, however, Ben Ali left the country and flew to Saudi Arabia. A gradual transition process was then initiated by the new prime minister and interim president, Mohammed Ghannouchi, which led to a number of government reshuffles. The first free elections were held on 23 October 2011.

Respect for human rights and support for democracy figure among the key themes in EU-Tunisia relations since the 1995 Association Agreement. In the preamble, the parties agree on the importance to be attached "to the principles of the United Nations Charter, particularly the observance of human rights and political and economic freedom, which form the very basis of the Association."[2] Article 2 also states that "relations between the Parties, as well as all the provisions of the Agreement itself, shall be based on respect for human rights and democratic principles which guide their domestic and international policies and constitute an essential element of the Agreement."[3] By the end of 2010, however, Tunisia was broadly seen as a nondemocratic state, with an average score of 6 out of 7 in the 2011 Freedom House democracy index ("not free"), and a score of −4 in the latest Polity IV democracy index ("autocracy").

When the revolution started, the EU could have resorted to at least two potentially relevant diplomatic tools in its bilateral relations with the Tunisian government. On the one hand, apart from benefiting from privileged trade arrangements, the EU allocated Tunisia approximately €300 million for the 2007–2010 period within the framework of the ENPI, and had promised further €240 million for the period 2011–2013. Therefore, by the time the revolt began, Tunisia was not just on the receiving end of a substantial amount of European funds, but was also at the crossing point between the two phases of the ENPI budget cycle. Furthermore, on 11 May 2010 the EU and Tunisia had begun negotiations towards upgrading the latter's status within the ENPI to "advanced status."[4] In May the parties set up an "ad hoc group" with the task of elaborating a "roadmap" for the process, and by the beginning of the protests in December 2010 the negotiations were still ongoing.[5] By December 2010, therefore, the EU had both economic and diplomatic tools available for making its voice heard by the Tunisian government.

Even if this context seems to correspond to the best-case scenarios depicted by scholars advocating a proactive use of conditionality by the EU in support of democratic reforms in its neighborhood, the EU's policy initiatives vis-à-vis the Tunisian government in the various phases of the revolution appear inconsistent and there is little evidence for their effectiveness in influencing the transition.

First of all, there is little if any evidence that the course of the Jasmine revolution between December 2010 and January 2011 was influenced by EU announcements and policy initiatives. The suddenness of the crisis and the pace at which it developed clearly took European leaders and EU Commissioners by surprise. When the EU did attempt to intervene, it did so quite late and—somehow surprisingly—in support of Ben Ali's regime, but with little or no impact on the course of events. On 10 January the High Representative for Foreign Affairs and Security Policy Catherine Ashton and the European Commissioner for Enlargement and Neighbourhood Policy Štefan Füle stated that the bloc's negotiations to upgrade relations with Tunis to "advanced status" would continue, but they would involve greater commitment to "human rights and fundamental freedoms."[6] A delegation of MEPs called on 12 January for an independent inquiry into the violence and for a suspension of the advanced status talks, but this was not followed up by any official initiative, also because on 14 January Ben Ali left the country.[7]

A chronologically broader look at the impact of the EU on the revolution offers a similar picture. Shortly before the revolution the EU had been under attack by a number of INGOs and think-tanks for not having responded to the adoption on 15 June 2010 by the Tunisian parliament of an amendment to the penal code which allowed for prosecution of "any persons who shall, directly or indirectly, have contacts with agents of a foreign country, foreign institution or organization in order to encourage them to affect the vital interests of Tunisia and its economic security." It was alleged that this amendment was approved after Tunisian human rights defenders held a meeting with EU officials in Madrid in April 2010 in the context of EU-Tunisia negotiations over granting Tunisia advanced partner status, and was rightly perceived as a potential threat to Tunisian NGOs and a windscreen for further violations of key human rights in the country.[8]

The use of economic tools in the aftermath of the revolution as a means to encourage and consolidate the democratic transition was also problematic. The EU allocated €17 million to cover the most urgent needs after the January events, but, more importantly, on 1 April Commissioner Füle promised to double the €160 million allocated to the country in the 2012–13 ENPI budget "in line with the ambitious reforms launched by the government that the Tunisian people will choose."[9] The strings attached to this diplomatic "carrot" were however made clear a few days later by European Commission chief Jose Manuel Barroso, who proposed an aid package which closely resembled Füle's—an extra €140 million, this time for the entire 2011–2013 period—provided that the Tunisian government took "strong and clear action" to curb illegal immigration to European countries.[10] The final aid package was approved by the European Commission on 24 August and amounted to €110 million[11] and was closely followed by a meeting between Füle and the Minister of the Interior of Tunisia in which they agreed, among other things, on a "dialogue" leading to the conclusion of a "mobility partnership with a view to establishing a mutually satisfactory cooperation on migration and mobility of people."[12]

In the aftermath of the revolution, EU officials also seemed at first reluctant to proceed with the negotiations on Tunisia's "advanced status." On 5 April Füle's spokesman stated that the resumption of negotiations on Tunisia's advanced status was "premature," and that they would be resumed in the future "with more permanent authorities" which "must agree to respect a range of criteria, which will enable us to assess the appropriateness of these negotiations."[13] This stance was later relaxed and, on 6 September, Füle "stressed the EU's readiness to restart negotiations with Tunisia on the 'Advanced Status' as soon as possible, in light of the political reforms being implemented in the country."[14] This decision could be associated both with steps taken by the Tunisian government to improve its human rights record—such as its decision, announced in June, to take part in three key international human rights conventions, a step defined by Ashton as a "clear signal" of Tunisia's new course[15]—and with the partial redefinition of EU's policy priorities announced by Ashton in May, when she called for the EU to "rise to the neighbourhood challenges."[16]

With some partial exceptions, during the Tunisian crisis EU Commissioners seemed to react to developments on the ground rather than impose any form of a democratic conditionality. The EU's stance, especially in the initial phases of the conflict, can be attributed to two main causes. On the one hand, even during the crisis few denied that the EU was under heavy pressure from member states —especially France, Spain, Italy, and Malta—not to undermine a government which was perceived as a bastion against Islamic radicalism and, most importantly, illegal immigration.[17] After the revolution, similar pressure was exerted to ensure that the new regime would commit itself on these two key points, as reflected by Barroso and Füle's statements issued in April on economic aid and the advanced status negotiations. Reports that Commissioner Füle gradually grew "exasperated" at the position of member states somehow confirm the intensity of the pressure experienced by the Commission during the revolution.[18]

However, the EU's policy towards Tunisia throughout the crisis reveals a second, perhaps more interesting problem—the deeper incompatibility of two key souls of the Neighbourhood Policy: state-building and democracy-building.[19] Since 2001, it has been clear that the EU has been interested in countries in its region being both stable and, if possible, democratic and respectful of key human rights. The latter goal was often stated in European Union documentation, but the creation of stable and effective governments in the region remained a key worry of the EU. For instance, article 87 of the 1995 EU-Tunisia agreement stated that "nothing in the agreement shall prevent a Contracting Party from taking any measures [. . .] which it considers essential to its own security in the event of serious internal disturbances affecting the maintenance of law and order."[20] In May 2010, when agreeing on the beginning of the negotiations over Tunisia's advanced status, Füle stated that EU-Tunisian relations were "excellent," and described Tunisia as "an important and reliable partner" and an "economic pioneer among European Union Neighbours."[21] The Jasmine Revolution, and more generally the Arab Spring, brought the inner tension within the Neighbourhood Policy to the surface. It made clear that no easy solution was forthcoming to the dilemma of how to approach a scenario in which a choice needs to be made between stability and democracy.

Libya between Humanitarian Intervention and "Effective Multilateralism"

The Libyan civil war is, to date, probably the most complex event within the Arab Spring. A first wave of protests erupted on 15 February 2011 after the arrest of a local activist; as revolts intensified in the following days, the regime led by Muammar Gaddafi cracked down on the protesters with increased violence. The rioters however gradually achieved control over key towns in the eastern side of the country, including Libya's second biggest city Benghazi, and on 27 February they established an interim government, the National Transitional Council (TNC). The revolts had by that time evolved into a full-fledged civil war, with rebels fighting for the control of a number of cities around the country, including Misrata, Brega, Ras Lanuf, and Bin Jawad. Reports of substantial civilian casualties, together with the prospect of the relatively imminent fall of the Gaddafi regime, convinced a number of Western countries to take sides in the conflict, calling for the imposition of a no-fly zone over the country to neutralize Gaddafi's forces and, albeit indirectly, help the advance of the rebel forces. On 17 March UNSCR 1973 was adopted, calling for an immediate ceasefire and authorizing the imposition of a no-fly zone, which was implemented initially by French and American forces on 19 March before NATO took command of the operation on 24 March. Gaddafi's regime opposed a strong resistance but eventually relinquished control of the Libyan capital Tripoli on 20 August, and finally collapsed on 20 October when the town of Sirte fell in rebel hands and Muammar Gaddafi was captured and killed.

From a political and diplomatic perspective, it is possible to credit certain senior EU officials in the early stages of the Libyan crisis with taking some valuable steps. For instance, one of the key turning points of the crisis—the resolution by the Arab League, passed on 12 March, in which it called for the UN Security Council to "take the necessary measures to impose immediately a no-fly zone on Libyan military aviation"—was preceded by statements by Catherine Ashton on 10 March stressing the importance of reaching a shared position "in conjunction with the Arab League" and of "them giving us a lead from the Arab world on what's happened."[22] This position is a rare example of senior EU officials approaching a crisis in the Middle East with a truly inter-regional spirit, in line with the principle of "effective multilateralism" which often emerges in post-9/11 EU policy documents such as the 2003 European Security Strategy.[23]

The attempt to put into practice the principle of "effective multilateralism" is even clearer after the beginning of the NATO intervention. Between 20 March and 25 April EU officials attended four multilateral conferences, two organized by EU member states (France and UK) and two organized respectively by the African Union and the Arab League; they also met bilaterally the heads of the African Union in Brussels and of the GCC in Abu Dhabi; and they joined the Contact Group on Libya, set up in London on 29 March, and maintained contacts with the AU High-Level Ad Hoc Committee on Libya.

Also, the EU acted proactively to secure an arms embargo over the country. On 25 February Catherine Ashton stated that it was time to consider "restrictive measures" against Libya[24] and on the same day 27 EU leaders agreed on an arms embargo, assets freezes and travel bans on Libyan senior officials; however, some countries (like Switzerland) had preceded the EU in announcing the assets freeze, and the agreement among EU countries was not "drafted legally" until after the approval of UNSCR 1970.[25] The relative keenness of European countries to implement the arms embargo is also compounded by the fact that up to that moment European countries had been by far the main providers of military equipment to Libya,[26] and that the strengthening of trade relations between European countries and Libya in the years that preceded the civil war did not correspond to any sensible improvement of its human rights record.

Some substantial questions, however, remain. On the one hand, especially after the endorsement of a no-fly zone by the Arab League and the approval of UNSCR 1973, the EU showed remarkable lack of leadership and did little more than endorse the initiatives of some of its member states—most notably France and the UK. It is indeed quite revealing that none of the four major summits held in the weeks that followed the beginning of military operations was hosted by the EU in Brussels, whereas the African Union and Arab League hosted one each.

The disappointment over Europe's failure to act in a decisive and effective way in the early phases of the crisis has been summarized by Sven Biscop, who considers the crisis in Libya as "a textbook example of a situation in which Europe, through the European Union, should have taken the lead and proved that it is an actor worth noting."[27] He remarked that in this crisis three key conditions for a forceful EU-led intervention were present—a UN mandate, support from the competent regional organization (the Arab League) and unwillingness on the part of the US to take the lead—and yet the EU did not succeed in "taking charge of crisis management" in Libya.

It is certainly worth noting that, as opposed to the Tunisian case—where the EU could count on an established legal framework for intervening in the crisis—the arguments of those advocating a stronger role of the EU in taking the lead in the Libyan crisis primarily rest on normative and, possibly, ethical grounds. However, Biscop is correct in highlighting that, broadly speaking, lack of "European unity"[28] over the modes and contents of external interventions into the affairs of Libya were by far the main cause of the inability of the EU to act effectively. In contrast to the Tunisian case, where (also because of the pace of the revolt) no major fracture emerged among key EU member states, in the Libyan crisis France and the UK actively supported a military intervention and convened two conferences in late March 2011, and other member states, notably Italy and Germany, maintained substantially more cautious positions.

The intensity of trade relations between Libya and European countries could account for the divisions within the EU as to which course of action to take in dealing with the Libyan civil war. Italy and Germany were in 2009 the two main markets for Libyan exports (accounting respectively for 20 percent and 8 percent of exports from Libya) and, also considering that most business contracts were negotiated directly with the Gaddafi family, were both initially skeptical about the prospect of siding with the rebels, with Italy eventually and somehow reluctantly joining France and the UK once a military intervention was seen as unavoidable. Italy had also signed in 2008 an important bilateral friendship and cooperation agreement with Libya that helped decrease the influx of illegal immigrants to Southern Italy; safeguarding this agreement was seen as a political priority by Berlusconi's right-wing coalition. The fact that both France and Britain had more diversified trade patterns with the region than Italy, and had a weaker economic interchange with Libya than Germany, partly account for their choice to take the lead in these diplomatic efforts. However, the decision of France and the UK to turn their backs on the Libyan regime at an early stage in the civil war was certainly influenced by the prospect of taking advantage of what was perceived and portrayed as humanitarian intervention to arouse strong domestic (and, especially in France, electoral) support for the governments in power. Similarly, the weak support for an international intervention among the German public and its politicians played a substantial role in influencing Germany's choice not to be involved in military operations.

Some of the later attempts made by the EU to bridge this divide and restore some degree of unity of intent under the European flag resulted in deeply misconceived initiatives. For instance, the creation of a German-led force under NATO's aegis—named EUFOR Libya—was announced on 1 April,[29] but its deployment was made conditional on a request by the UN Office for the Co-ordination of Humanitarian Affairs (OCHA), which never came.[30] This episode confirmed that the Council perceived the necessity of some form of EU-coordinated intervention in the country, but also showed the lack of clear planning and, possibly, the lack of diplomatic leverage vis-à-vis other major multilateral actors, such as the UN Secretary General.

Conclusion

It is objectively difficult to draw from these two episodes clear lessons as to how the EU could have acted more effectively to encourage or facilitate the democratic transitions in the context of the Arab Spring. The reasons why the EU as an institution struggled to have a recognizable impact on the Tunisian revolution and the Libyan civil war can mostly be attributed to the disagreements among its member states on the desirability of Ben Ali's and Gaddafi's regimes collapsing (and, especially, collapsing *abruptly*). The existence of mutually beneficial bilateral agreements between these countries and key EU member states largely accounts for the problems faced by EU institutions in expressing convincing leadership during the early phases of the Arab Spring, and reveals a number of inconsistencies that can hardly be explained on purely ideological or ethical grounds. France, for instance, had privileged political and economic relations with Tunisia and is its main trade partner, with bilateral exchanges worth $9 billion in 2010, but Libya exported to Germany and Italy respectively twice and five times as much oil as to France. France's interest in the maintenance of the status quo in Tunisia and its comparatively weak links with Libya seem to explain better than any broader ideological or ethical consideration why it defended the principle of "non-interference" during the Tunisian revolution, but was at the forefront of the international military campaign during the Libyan war.[31]

However, it is possible to suggest that the Tunisian revolution and the Libyan civil war highlighted the need for decisive action in three directions. European countries and the EU as an institution need, first of all, to reassess the priorities in their bilateral and multilateral relations with Arab countries. The resilience of Middle Eastern authoritarian regimes meant that, before the Arab Spring, few in Europe perceived the necessity of choosing *in practice* between promoting stability and democracy in the region; today, however, the fact that democratic change has become a real option called for European institutions and countries to take clear steps in defense of democratic movements and reforms whenever the prospect of such changes occurs.

The management of the Tunisian and Libyan crises, and the attempts to reach a unified position at the European level to support democratic transitions, were also thwarted by the absence of a common position on how to manage migration fluxes from North Africa. Action to address this problem should be taken at two different levels. On the one hand, it is imperative that, in case of an objective emergency, European countries share the responsibility of managing sudden bursts in the influx of illegal migrants; the vocal and justified criticism by countries like Italy and Malta towards their northern neighbors was one of the factors that further complicated decision-making processes within EU bodies between March and April 2011. Also, the crisis highlighted the need for EU member states to agree on a common asylum policy for the Union as soon as possible, and not later than 2012 as currently planned.

The argument on whether the EU should have shown leadership in the *military* operations in Libya is more complex. The ability to timely deploy an EU-coordinated peacekeeping force could be an important asset towards playing a role in complex transition processes that evolve into civil wars, as in the Libyan case, but for the time being little agreement exists on the desirability of such operations taking place under an EU flag. However, one of the lessons that can be drawn from the Libyan case is that, when a decision is taken to deploy a specific military operation, the credibility of the EU as an international actor is at stake. The fact that the EU-FOR Libya initiative was considered by some an "April fool's joke"[32] certainly did not contribute to raising the profile of the EU vis-à-vis the transitional council, and the absence of an EU-led military initiative during the civil will probably not allow the EU to position itself as a relevant actor in the early phases of democratic transition.

Notes

1. Council of the European Union, "Consolidated Versions of the Treaty on European Union and the Treaty on the Functioning of the European Union," Brussels, April 15, 2008, accessed October 17, 2011, http://register.consilium.europa.eu/pdf/en/08/st06/st06655.en08.pdf.

2. European Union-Tunisia, "Euro-Mediterranean Agreement Establishing an Association between the European Communities and their Member States, of the One Part, and the Republic of Tunisia, of the Other Part," Brussels, July 17, 1995, accessed October 17, 2011, http://eur-lex.europa.eu/LexUriServ/LexUriServ.do?uri=CELEX:21998A0330(01):ES:HTML.

3. Ibid.

4. ENPI Information Centre, "EU and Tunisia Agree to Work Towards Advanced Status," May 11, 2010, accessed October 17, 2011, http://www.enpi-info.eu/mainmed.php?id_type=1&id=21537.

5. Ibid.

6. Leigh Phillips, "Mediterranean EU States Block Stronger Action on Tunisia," EUobserver.com, January 14, 2011, accessed October 17, 2011, http://euobserver.com/24/31644.

7. ENPI Information Centre, "Tunisia: European Parliament Delegation Calls for Independent Inquiry into Deadly Riots," January 12, 2011, accessed October 17, 2011, http://www.enpi-info.eu/mainmed.php?id=23720&id_type=1&lang_id=450.

8. Human Rights Watch, "World Report 2011: Tunisia," accessed October 17, 2011, http://www.hrw.org/world-report-2011/tunisia.

9. ENPI Information Centre, "Extra EU Aid to Tunisia: This Is Just the Beginning," April 1, 2011, accessed October 17, 2011, http://www.enpi-info.eu/mainmed.php?id=24735&id_type=1&lang_id=450.

10. Valentina Pop, "Barroso to Tunisia: More Money If You Want Your Migrants Back," EUobserver.com, April 13, 2011, accessed October 17, 2011, http://euobserver.com/9/32169.

11. ENPI Information Centre, "Annual Action Programme 2011: EU Aid to Support the Economic and Political Transition Process in Tunisia," August 24, 2011, accessed October 17, 2011, http://www.enpi-info.eu/mainmed.php?lang_id=450&searchtype=simple&id=26095&id_type=1.

12. European Commission, "Statement by Commissioner Stefan Füle Following His Meeting with Mr Habib Essid, Minister of Interior of Tunisia," Brussels, September 6, 2011, accessed October 17, 2011,

http://europa.eu/rapid/pressReleasesAction.do?reference=MEMO/11/582&format=HTML&aged=0&language=EN&guiLanguage=en.

13. ANSAmed, "Tunisia: EU Commission, Advanced Status Talks Premature," April 5, 2011, accessed October 17, 2011, http://www.ansamed.info/en/news/ME.XEF21750.html.

14. European Commission, "Statement by Commissioner Stefan Füle Following His Meeting with Mr Habib Essid."

15. ENPI Information Centre, "Ashton Hails Clear Signal as Tunisia Signs Up for Key Human Rights Conventions," July 4, 2011, accessed October 17, 2011, http://www.enpi-info.eu/mainmed.php?lang_id=4 50&searchtype=simple&id=25782&id_type=1.

16. ENPI Information Centre, "Ashton: EU Needs to Rise to the Neighbourhood Challenges," May 11, 2011, accessed October 17, 2011, http://www.enpi-info.eu/mainmed.php?lang_id=450&searchtype=si mple&id=25156&id_type=1

17. Leigh Phillips, "Mediterranean EU States Block Stronger Action on Tunisia," *EUObserver.com*, January 14, 2011, http://euobserver.com/24/31644.

18. Ibid.

19. Gorm Rye Olsen, "Europe and the Promotion of Democracy in Post Cold War Africa: How Serious Is Europe and For What Reason?" *African Affairs* 97, no. 388 (1998): 343–67.

20. European Union-Tunisia, "Euro-Mediterranean Agreement."

21. ENPI Information Centre, "EU and Tunisia Agree to Work towards Advanced Status."

22. "Arab League to Guide on Libya Rebels—EU's Ashton," *Reuters*, March 10, 2011, accessed October 17, 2011, http://af.reuters.com/article/worldNews/idAFTRE7296XF20110310.

23. Council of the European Union, "A Secure Europe in a Better World: The European Security Strategy," Brussels, December 12, 2003, 9. Accessed October 17, 2011, http://www.consilium.europa.eu/uedocs/cmsUpload/78367.pdf.

24. Council of the European Union, "Remarks by High Representative, Catherine Ashton on Libya in the Margins of the Informal Defence Ministerial Meeting," Brussels, February 25, 2011, accessed October 17, 2011, http://www.consilium.europa.eu/uedocs/cms_data/docs/pressdata/EN/foraff/119502.pdf.

25. "Government Denies that Sanctions Have Been Agreed," *The Times of Malta*, February 25, 2011, accessed October 17, 2011, http://www.timesofmalta.com/articles/view/20110225/local/eu-agrees-first-anti-gaddafi-sanctions.351990.

26. "EU Arms Exports to Libya: Who Armed Gaddafi?" *The Guardian*, March 1, 2011, accessed October 17, 2011, http://www.guardian.co.uk/news/datablog/2011/mar/01/eu-arms-exports-libya.

27. Sven Biscop, "Mayhem in the Mediterranean: Three Strategic Lessons for Europe," Egmont—Royal Institute for International Relations, Security Policy Brief, No. 19 (April 2011), 1.

28. Ibid.

29. Council of the European Union, "Council Decision 2011/210/CFSP of 1 April 2011," accessed October 17, 2011, http://eur-lex.europa.eu/LexUriServ/LexUriServ.do?uri=OJ:L:2011:089:0017:0020:en:PDF.

30. Ana Gomes, "Was Eufor Libya an April Fool's Joke?" *EUobserver.com*, July 13, 2011, accessed October 17, 2011, http://euobserver.com/7/32624.

31. Steven Erlanger, "France Seen Wary of Interfering in Tunisia Crisis," *The New York Times*, January 16, 2011, accessed October 17, 2011, http://www.nytimes.com/2011/01/17/world/africa/17france.html.

32. Gomes, "Was Eufor Libya an April Fool's Joke?"

4

Egypt

Michelle Pace

Egypt is a major trading partner of the EU in its southern Mediterranean neighborhood. The EU-Egypt Association Agreement of 2004 established a free-trade area between the two partners. An agreement on agricultural, processed agricultural and fisheries products was put in force in June 2010 and there have been ongoing negotiations to improve conditions for services trade and for companies seeking to establish businesses in both markets. Despite the global slowdown, total EU-Egypt bilateral trade volume reached its highest level ever in 2010 (22 billion Euros).[1]

Other factors make Egypt a crucial ally of the European Union (and the West) in the Middle East and North African sphere: Egypt is the most populous country in the Middle East and the third-most populous on the African continent (its population size as of April 2011 stood at 82,999,393). Its political influence within the Non-Aligned Movement and the African Union stems from, amongst others, its strategic geographical position, its diplomatic expertise, its military strength and historical events. The Arab League was formed in Cairo in 1945. Moreover, Egypt's role and efforts in the Middle East peace process since Camp David (1978) is also a crucial factor in its relationship with the EU. Egypt has traditionally perceived itself as a regional power and wants neighboring countries and international observers to see it that way too. Historically, this perception is due to the legacy of Nasser, but in more recent times Egyptian attempts to mediate between Israel and the Palestinians have been a main source of legitimacy for its role. Egyptian officials have often seen themselves as the only "natural" mediators and have been very keen to maintain and protect this role from challenges emanating from Turkey and at times even Qatar and Saudi Arabia. The EU has wholly supported the Egyptian government's mediation efforts including those between the two main rival factions in the Occupied Palestinian Territory—Fatah and Hamas. In 2011, Egypt opened the Gaza border crossing, allowing Palestinians a lifeline after four years of border closure. Given this background, it is no surprise that the EU has been struggling to juggle between its economic and strategic interests on the one hand and its declared wish to see democratization and respect for human rights in Egypt on the other hand.

This chapter attempts to tease out the role that the EU has played in promoting human rights and democracy in Egypt through its various bilateral (including the European Neighbourhood Policy or ENP), and multilateral, regional (the Euro-Mediterranean Partnership or EMP/the Union for the Mediterranean or UfM)[2] initiatives. In so doing, it analyzes the effectiveness or otherwise of these strategies. It then moves on to assess the response of the EU to events and protests as they developed in Egypt from January 2011 to the present day. It concludes by making some tentative suggestions as to whether there are any lessons to be learned from these recent events for EU policy-making and which steps the EU needs to take in light of these developments.

Role of the EU in Promoting Human Rights and Democracy in Egypt: Effectiveness and Ineffectiveness of These Policies

Since the initiation of bilateral relations with Egypt, through a cooperation agreement in 1976, the European Union (EU) has opted for a strategy which ensures stability and security, at least in the short term, in the most important neighboring country in the Arab-Mediterranean region. At the same time, particularly since the launching in 1995 of the Euro-Mediterranean Partnership (EMP), the EU has attempted to cautiously pursue a strategy of promoting human rights and democracy, without upsetting the ruling, authoritarian regime in Egypt. The latter it has tried to achieve through the promotion of political dialogue and the funding of co-opted NGOs (that is, institutions close to the Mubarak regime) such as the National Council for Women whose President was First Lady Suzanne Mubarak.[3] A representative from the EU Delegation in Cairo disagrees. The interviewee in question argued that:

> The National Council for Childhood and Motherhood, the National Council for Women as well as the National Council for Human Rights are not co-opted NGOs. They are national bodies established by the Government of Egypt and, often supported by the EU under the ENP. For example, note the creation of an Ombudsman at the NCHR. These national bodies functioned like local NGOs in that they "channelled" EU support to local NGOs and civil society organizations working in their sector of responsibility, that is, human rights, women's issues, etc. . . . I believe that the process of award/funds allocation from these bodies was affected by the nature of the issues and the nature of the NGO. This is certainly true of the NCHR. Nevertheless and from my experience at the delegation, the NCW and the NCCM specifically are seen in more positive terms by EC officials, at least with regards to the bodies' influence on legislation and change. For example, note the Council's role in the establishment of the Child Law of 2008 and Egyptian efforts at passing the first anti-harassment law, as well as efforts to address the issue of eradicating female genital mutilation.[4]

Although the EU-Egypt Association Agreement of 2004 provided a legal basis for relations, particularly via Article 2, the EU never confronted the ruling Mubarak regime in cases of severe violations of human rights. Instead, its preference was for a continued economic, political and social partnership with the authoritarian government of Egypt. Article 2 of the EU-Egypt

Association Agreement clearly stipulates that respect for human rights and democracy constitutes an "essential element" of EU-Egypt relations (which incorporates the EU's earlier financial tool for supporting the implementation of the EMP, that is, the MEDA programme).

Ironically, while Egypt was concluding its Association Agreement with the EU, on the same day, the People's Assembly adopted a new law which President Mubarak ratified on Civil Associations and Institutions (Law 153 of 1999) and which severely restricts freedom of association. As Barbara Cochrane Alexander argues,

> Despite the elimination of 22 clauses that had given the Egyptian Government broad power over NGOs, certain significant restrictions still remain in Law No. 153. For example, the government has the power to "object to whatever it deems as contradictory to [Egyptian] law in the statute of the association" (Part I, Chapter I, Article 8). In addition, Law No. 153 bans NGO participation in political or trade union activities or any activities that "[t]hreaten national unity, violate public order or morality" (Part I, Chapter II, Article 11). It also grants the government the power to determine which non-Egyptian organizations an association may join (Part I, Chapter II, Article 16). Finally, Law No. 153 prohibits organizations from accepting foreign funding (Part I, Chapter II, Article 17). Violations of any of these articles enable the government to dissolve the association after a court hearing (Part I, Chapter IV, Article 42).[5]

So, while the EU Council welcomed the successful conclusions of the negotiations between the EU and Egypt, Egypt breached its international commitments by adopting the new law.[6] Apart from the signing of the EU-Egypt Association Agreement, which was formally supposed to strengthen Egypt's commitment to upholding universal human rights,[7] Egypt had previously ratified the International Covenant on Civil and Political Rights which should, in theory at least, also guarantee freedom of association as enshrined in Article 22.

Yet, since the launching of the EMP or Barcelona Process in 1995, the human rights situation in Egypt has deteriorated rapidly. Serious human rights violations have been reported by various international NGOs including the Euro-Mediterranean Human Rights Network, the International Federation of Human Rights Leagues, the Human Rights Watch, Amnesty International, etc.[8] Despite all these reports, the EU has never openly challenged the Egyptian government on these issues within the context of the Euro-Mediterranean Partnership or the ENP for that matter—although there has been a varied response from EU actors in foreign policy making. For instance, the European Parliament was not as "soft" in its responses to serious human rights violations in Egypt as the Commission was.[9] Moreover, the various interests and relations (commercial and political) of individual EU member states with southern Mediterranean countries have been the main issue hindering the potential for any coherent EU strategy to push political reforms forward within the EMP framework, that is to apply political conditionality in Egypt.[10]

Following the events of 9/11, EU Member States intensified their cooperation with Egypt in their proclaimed fight against terrorism, to secure a "peaceful" neighborhood, manage immigration flows, at the same time as they enhanced their trade relations. Issues pertaining to the promotion of respect for human rights and political reform/democratization were placed on the back burner. The EU's main leverage, its financial assistance packages, was in fact mainly distributed to programs dealing with economic issues, immigration-control, security cooperation and the fight against terrorism.

The launching of the European Neighbourhood Policy (ENP) in 2003 was supposed to herald a new beginning in EU-Mediterranean relations. The EU's enlargement to the East (and South) opened up further opportunities for the EU to "deepen" its relations with its neighbors. The EU-Egypt ENP Action Plan, approved in March 2007 for a period of three to five years, acknowledges that the deepening in EU-Egypt relations is mainly aimed at the economic sphere in order to ensure stability and security on Europe's southern borders.

> Egypt continues to pursue its dynamic foreign policy aimed at strengthening its relations with its international partners in particular the EU, its commitment *to further integration with*

> *the global economy*, and its efforts *to further political and economic*
> *development and modernization*. Thus, a major opportunity has
> evolved for Egypt and the EU to further develop *their stra-*
> *tegic partnership* through an increasingly close and enhanced
> relationship. This will involve *a significant degree of economic*
> *integration* and deepening of political, cultural and social co-
> operation, aiming to promote peace, *stability, security, growth*,
> development, and prosperity in the Euro-Mediterranean re-
> gion as well as *modernization of the Egyptian economy and society*
> (own emphasis).[11]

Somehow the logic that economic development will automati-
cally lead to political change persists in the EU psyche. In terms
of Egypt's political reforms, especially the protection of human
rights and fundamental freedoms, the ENP is very vague about
what exactly the EU aims to achieve.[12] In the carefully worded
EU-Egypt Action Plan document, the EU simply states that:

> the Action Plan aims to support such efforts and priorities
> as reflected in the National Development Plan 2002–2007,
> President Mubarak's Electoral Platform for 2005 and the Gov-
> ernment's statement to the parliament in January 2006 (own
> emphasis).[13]

As Michael Emerson reflects, the political stagnation in Egypt
and elsewhere "in the Southern Mediterranean has now been
overturned by the Arab Spring, but not thanks to the ENP,
whose actions were largely supporting the status quo."[14]

In 2008, the EU's Mediterranean policy was resuscitated
through the Union for the Mediterranean (or UfM).[15] Egypt had
(and officially still has) a very prominent role in this new initiative—it held the co-presidency together with France. French
President Nicolas Sarkozy's ambitious UfM project emphasized
the need to focus on economic development of the southern Mediterranean—as a pre-emptive effort to "manage" immigration
flows and secure stability in and around Europe. The increasing
securitization of the Mediterranean (especially since the events of
9/11), the global economic crisis and the complicated politics of
the region, all overshadowed principled issues of the protection

of human rights and the promotion of democracy in the Southern Mediterranean. Euro-Mediterranean cooperation in the field of anti-terrorism legislation has in fact, since 9/11, intensified at the expense of civil liberties.[16] Thus the UfM has proven unable to meet the basic needs of the peoples of the southern Mediterranean or to live up to the expectations of the international community.

The EU's Response to Events and Protests in Egypt since January 2011

The popular uprising that began in Egypt on 25 January 2011 was driven as much by frustrated economic aspirations as by repressed political aspirations. The results of the 2010 Egyptian legislative elections left a deep sense of frustration and discontent amongst opposition groups and much of the Egyptian population. The Shura Council elections of June and the People's Assembly elections (28 November and 5 December) were deemed irregular by Egyptian opposition groups as well as local and international rights groups.[17] The EU's response was a rhetorical one, with Lady Catherine Ashton declaring:

> Ahead of these elections we took positive note of the measures of the Government and the Higher Electoral Commission to increase transparency in the election process including local election observation. Unfortunately the implementation of these measures was insufficient. I was *concerned* by reports of irregularities, restricted access for independent observers and candidates' representatives into polling stations, media restrictions as well as arrests of opposition activists.
>
> A significant segment of the opposition withdrew after the first round of the elections. I particularly *regret* the incidents of violence, some of them resulting in loss of life.
>
> I *encourage* the Egyptian authorities to respond to these concerns. The EU will continue to call on the Egyptian government to permit domestic and international monitors to observe future elections, and remains ready to offer assistance in that regard.
>
> Egypt is a key partner of the EU and we remain committed to continue working together, building on the reforms already

undertaken and on the programme set out in the EU/Egypt
Action Plan (own emphasis).[18]

The EU has thus excluded the possibility of sanctioning Egypt
(or any other Southern Mediterranean state for that matter) for
failing to respect the principles of human rights and democracy
that the two partners are supposed to "share." Rather, the EU
has always preferred the soft option of positive conditionality,
arguing that dialogue works better than sanctions. At times,
when the EU appeared to adopt a more open diplomatic discourse on human rights in the Mediterranean, this discourse
was clearly very selective and unbalanced. So, for example, although the EU adopted the Communication on *"Reinvigorating
EU actions on human rights and democratisation with Mediterranean
partners"* on 21 May 2003 with ten concrete recommendations,[19]
it undertook very few steps with regard to actually implementing these recommendations.

Thus, at this stage (post 2010 elections in Egypt), the EU appeared to be unable and unwilling (especially from the part of
some of its Member States) to appreciate the deep grievances
amongst Egyptians with regard to police abuse and torture, state
of emergency laws, uncontrollable corruption, high unemployment, food price inflation, absence of a minimum wage, lack of
free elections and freedom of speech.[20]

Eventually, the protests in Tunisia (which were sparked by
the self-immolation of Mohamed Bouazizi on 17 December, 2010
and which led to the ousting of President Zine El Abidine Ben
Ali on 14 January, 2011), inspired Egyptians to rise up against
their authoritarian ruler. They demanded an end to Mubarak's
regime and emergency law, freedom, justice, a share in the management and wealth of Egypt's resources and a (non-military)
government responsive to their needs. (Mubarak resigned from
office on 11th February.) Egypt's military establishment was
also put under pressure by the United States to force Mubarak
out. Europe took its time to respond. EU diplomats argue that,
unlike the United States, EU foreign policy represents a consensus between 27 member states, which makes it very difficult to
respond rapidly in one voice.[21] At the 2–3 February, 2011 Euro-

pean Parliament debate, EU foreign policy chief, Catherine Ashton, delivered a rather low-key speech, simply concluding that: "As the European Union, our offer to the region and its people is *solidarity and support* to put reforms in place. EU is a union of democracies—we have a democratic calling. So we will *back this process of change*, with patience, creativity and determination."[22]

Coming from the EU, which has a priority commitment in all its agreements with Egypt to promote democracy and human rights, this underwhelming response concerned many observers, including members of the European Parliament. Reflecting debates within the European Parliament and drawing a parallel to the events in Europe in 1989, Guy Verhofstadt of the ALDE group expressed disappointment that Europe had "failed to give support to the people in the street." Europe had made two errors: "We haven't really taken measure of this historic moment in time and we have failed to analyse the situation properly," he said. He called on the High Representative to change the EU's position. "The EU should stand 100 percent behind the Egyptian people and its demands. Mubarak should leave his country to democracy," he concluded.[23]

After Mubarak's resignation from office, the EU acknowledged that it needed a new approach "to strengthen the partnership between the EU and the countries and societies of the neighborhood: to build and consolidate healthy democracies, pursue sustainable economic growth and manage cross-border links."[24] In March 2011, it launched its "Partnership for Democracy and Shared Prosperity with the Southern Mediterranean,"[25] which was followed in May by its review of the ENP. What is striking about these initiatives is that there is nothing new in the EU's approach to its southern neighborhood. More financial assistance is deemed to be the answer "to the upheaval and democratic aspiration currently being seen in North Africa" . . . "On top of the 5.7 billion Euros already allocated for the period 2011–2013, additional funding of 1.24 billion Euros has been transferred from other existing resources, and will now be made available in support of the ENP." Moreover, the European Council agreed to increase European Investment Bank lending to the southern Mediterranean by 1 billion Euros over the same period.[26] The "more funds for more reform" approach advocated by Ashton and Commissioner Füle stops short of giving details on how the transition and new governments in the southern Mediterranean as well as the EU itself are going to ensure mutual accountability. Furthermore, there is no mention in this new initiative of how the EU is going to support "the development of deep democracy" in the neighborhood.

Lessons Learned? The Future of EU-Egypt Relations

If the EU is to have any influence in Egypt's transition to democracy it has to start by restoring its credibility. For decades, the EU happily supported the Mubarak regime in order to ensure stability and security in its southern neighborhood. This it has done at the expense of respect for human rights and civil liberties. In fact, the EU's approach relied far too heavily on a top-down approach in its assistance and promotion of democracy, and ignored bottom-up channels directed at organic civil society groups. Commissioner Štefan Füle himself acknowledged that the EU's stability-first approach, which required the support of Mubarak's corrupt and authoritarian regime, failed as it was too short-term focused:

> We must show humility about the past. Europe was not vocal enough in defending human rights and local democratic forces in the region. Too many of us fell prey to the assumption that authoritarian regimes were a guarantee of stability in the region. This was not even Realpolitik. It was, at best, short-termism—and the kind of short-termism that makes the long term ever more difficult to build.[27]

The ENP Review, however, does not augur well for those hoping for a change of track in the EU's approach towards Egypt and the southern neighbors. The ENP was due for a review in any case but it was postponed to coincide with the EU's reaction to the Arab Spring. When the Review was launched in May 2011 it promised more of the same old strategies in response to the events in the Arab world.[28] For example, the EU promises a "new approach" towards its neighborhood which aims to: "provide greater support to partners engaged in building deep democracy" and which must "be based on mutual accountability and a shared commitment to the universal values of human rights, democracy and the rule of law." However, there is no explanation how the EU aims to go "deeper" in its engagement with sub-state actors in neighboring countries or how the EU can be made accountable to Middle Eastern and North African (MENA) citizens.

So the only lesson that the EU seems to have learned from the upheaval in the Arab neighborhood thus far is how to continue with the same old rhetoric and same old means (mainly, making more additional funds available, through its "more funds for more reform" approach).

Egyptians claim that they are now working their way towards a civil state. Civil society groups continue to be financially supported by Egyptian businessmen.[29] Egyptians have refused IMF and World Bank lending packages.[30] However, the Supreme Council of the Egyptian Armed Forces (SCAF) continues to maintain patronage networks and is considering amendments to Egypt's existing electoral laws that may benefit former members of the now-disbanded National Democratic Party. If members of the former ruling party reenter political life in the guise of independent candidates, this would be an affront to many Egyptian revolutionaries who have been seeking to purge Egypt's institutions of remnants of the former Mubarak regime.[31]

Meanwhile, the EU has enough on its plate to keep it busy for some months to come. This so-called second wave of the Eurozone crisis is accompanied by the downgrade of America's credit rating (at time of writing). The EU has much to get in order in its own house. In terms of its foreign policy, the art for the future will be in how to navigate the two key interests of the EU: that is, stability on the one hand, and the support of democratic transitions in Egypt and across the MENA on the other.[32] In Tahrir Square, the best that protestors are hoping for from the forthcoming Egyptian elections (expected during the last two weeks of November) is a coalition which includes the

Muslim Brotherhood's Freedom and Justice Party.[33] Political opposition forces are not too keen on seeing the EU's observation mission in Egypt around the time of these elections. (In fact, international observers are ruled out.) Thus, the EU would be well advised to take a step back while the democratic transition in Egypt takes its course. As one interviewee put it, it may take one or two generations for real democracy to ensue in Egypt.[34] It follows that the EU has to move away from its negotiated documents (with the Mubarak government of the past), which say very little about the actions needed by both parties to the agreement to ensure full respect for human rights and a positive transformation of the political landscape into a democracy. Egypt's transition phase will be a very risky journey and it would probably be best for the EU to encourage a reliable transition process but not interfere in Egyptian affairs unless called to do so by the transition government.[35] Such calls will most likely take the shape of training programs for the new (especially youth) movements and political parties[36] seeking to learn more about democratic transition processes, reconciliation processes, building up an accountable and transparent police force and the re-formulation of Egypt's executive, judiciary and legislature.

It is important for the EU to bear in mind that Egypt's population is expected to double in 30–40 years' time. It makes sense therefore to look out for those candidates to Egypt's parliament or presidential elections who lay out a clear plan as to how to remedy the enormous pressure that this fact will put on Egypt's economy and society in terms of food, water, housing, education, general welfare, environment and energy resources. The EU would do well to encourage discussions on the gravity of this situation for Egypt's future, especially state and private developers and entrepreneurs who have it in their power to reverse the lack of responsible action of Mubarak's regime in these domains. What Egypt needs now is to look at its transition period as a whole. The creation of a commission to oversee the restructuring of Egypt's political, economic and social landscapes in the coming months and years[37] should be wholeheartedly supported by the EU.

Notes

1. Interview by the author with an official from a member state's embassy in Cairo, July 28, 2011. See also: European Commission, "Egypt," accessed October 23, 2011, http://ec.europa.eu/trade/creating-opportunities/bilateral-relations/countries/egypt/.

2. Despite attempts by the Commission to sell the UfM as a continuation/evolution of the EMP, these two policies are not the same in terms of rationale and structure.

3. Interview by the author with an Egyptian youth protestor, Cairo, July 28, 2011.

4. Interview by the author with an official from the EU Delegation in Cairo, July 28, 2011. See also "Egypt Moves Closer to Passing Sexual Harassment Laws," Reuters, accessed October 23, 2011, http://www.reuters.com/article/2010/02/17/us-egypt-harassment-idUSTRE61G3ZS20100217 and "Media Backgrounder: Female Genital Mutilation/ Cutting (FGM/C) Egypt," UNICEF, accessed October 23, 2011, http://www.unicef.org/egypt/media_4115.html.

5. See Barbara Cochrane Alexander, "Law No. 153: Its Impact on Egyptian Non-Governmental Organizations," *Human Rights Brief* 7, no. 2 (2000), accessed October 23, 2011, http://www.wcl.american.edu/hrbrief/07/2law153.cfm.

6. Euro-Mediterranean Human Rights Network, "Freedom of Association and Human Rights Organizations in Egypt," accessed October 23, 2011, http://www.euromedrights.org/en/publications-en/emhrn-publications/emhrn-publications-1999/3588.html.

7. "Although the main rationale of the AA was trade liberalisation, so the upholding of universal human rights was not enshrined as an exclusive goal," insists an official from the EU delegation in Cairo. Interview by the author, Cairo, July 28, 2011.

8. See for example the annual reports published by these international NGOs on violations of Human Rights in Egypt, some earlier and the most recent can be found here: Euro-Mediterranean Human Rights Network, "Freedom of Association and Human Rights Organizations in Egypt," accessed October 23, 2011, http://www.euromedrights.org/files/emhrn-publications/Freedom-of-Association-and-Human-Rights-Organisations-in-Egypt.pdf; Amnesty International, "Egypt Annual Report 2011," accessed October 23, 2011, http://www.amnesty.org/en/region/egypt/report-2011 and Human Rights Watch, "World Report 2011: Egypt,," accessed October 23, 2011, http://www.hrw.org/en/world-report-2011/egypt.

9. See for example European Parliament. "Joint Motion for a Resolution," accessed October 23, 2011, http://www.europarl .europa.eu/sides/getDoc.do?type=MOTION&reference=P6-RC-2008-0023&language=EN.

10. Interview with an EU official, Cairo, July 27, 2011 and another separate interview with an official from the EU delegation in Cairo, July 28, 2011.

11. European Commission, "EU-Egypt Action Plan,," accessed October 23, 2011, http://trade.ec.europa.eu/doclib/docs/2010/april/tradoc_146097.pdf.

12. Interview with an EU official, Cairo, July 27, 2011.

13. Ibid.

14. Michael Emerson, "Review of the Review—of the European Neighbourhood Policy," *Centre for European Policy Studies* 1 (2011).

15. The name of this initiative was eventually confirmed as "Barcelona Process: Union for the Mediterranean" (Council of the European Union 2008) to emphasize that the UfM revitalizes and complements rather than replaces the EMP. See Michelle Pace, "The EU and the Mediterranean," in *The European Union and Global Governance: A Handbook*, ed. David J. Bailey and Jens-Uwe Wunderlich (London: Routledge, 2011), 304–12.

16. Tobias Schumacher, "From Paris with Love?—Euro-Mediterranean Dynamics in the Light of French Ambitions," *The GCC-EU Research Bulletin* 10 (2008).

17. "Egyptian Elections: Opposition Alleges Fraud," *Guardian Weekly*, November 29, 2010, accessed October 23, 2011, http://www .guardian.co.uk/world/2010/nov/29/egyptian-opposition-alleges-election-fraud. See also, Human Rights Watch, "Elections in Egypt," accessed October 23, 2011, http://www.hrw.org/en/node/94512/section/4.

18. "Statement by EU High Representative Catherine Ashton on the Elections to the People's Assembly of Egypt," European Union, accessed October 23, 2011, http://www.consilium.europa.eu/uedocs/cms_data/docs/pressdata/EN/foraff/118243.pdf.

19. European Commission Communication, "Reinvigorating EU actions on Human Rights and Democratisation with Mediterranean Partners: Strategic Guidelines," Brussels, May 21, 2003, COM (2003) 294 final.

20. Although the EU has addressed these issues in the political sub-committees under the ENP and EU concerns have been explicitly articulated in the Annual ENP reports, the EU has been unable to

exercise any influence in the areas of democracy and human rights as defined above.

21. Interview with an EU official, Cairo, July 27, 2011.

22. "Remarks on Egypt and Tunisia," Catherine Ashton speech to the European Parliament, February 2, Speech/11/66, http://europa .eu/rapid/pressReleasesAction.do?reference=SPEECH/11/66&forma t=HTML&aged=0&language=EN&guiLanguage=en, accessed January 12, 2012.

23. European Parliament, "Brussels Plenary Session," accessed October 23, 2011, http://www.europarl.europa.eu/pdfs/news/public/ focus/20110131FCS12843/20110131FCS12843_en.pdf.

24. European Commission Communication, "A New Response to A Changing Neighbourhood," Brussels, May252011, COM(2011) 303 final: 1.

25. European Commission Communication, "A Partnership for Democracy and Shared Prosperity With the Southern Mediterranean," Brussels, March 8, 2011, COM(2011) 200 final.

26. EEAS and European Commission, "A New and Ambitious European Neighbourhood Policy," Brussels, May 25, 2011, IP/11/643.

27. "Speech on the Recent Events in North Africa," Štefan Füle, accessed October 23, 2011, http://europa.eu/rapid/ pressReleasesAction.do?reference=SPEECH/11/130.

28. European Commission Communication, "A New Response to a Changing Neighbourhood,." Brussels, May 25, 2011, COM(2011) 303 final.

29. Interview with a youth protestor, Cairo, July 28, 2011. Businessmen have been supporting civil society groups in Egypt for many years in an attempt to gain an image of "doing something for society." See for example the Sawiris Foundation, accessed October 23, 2011, http:// www.sawirisfoundation.org/. The very same actors are still active today but the Egyptian business elite is in a huge flux now: some are in prison while the majority managed to retain their business empires, at least for the time being. But the key message from this interviewee is that the EU should not get involved in Egypt unless asked by Egyptians for support.

30. Patrick Werr, "Egypt Rejection of IMF Cash may Slow Recovery," *thedailynewsegypt*.com, June 28, 2011, accessed November 4, 2011, http://www.thedailynewsegypt.com/economy/egypt-rejection -of-imf-cash-may-slow-recovery.html.

31. Jeremy M. Sharp, "Egypt in Transition," accessed October 18, 2011, http://www.crs.gov.

32. Interview with an EU official, Cairo, July 27, 2011.

33. At the time of submitting this chapter, the political scenario is changing once more with a new "liberal" coalition (of liberal, leftist, Coptic and, for the first time, Sufi political parties, groups and associations) emerging from parties included in the Democratic Alliance. This seems to confirm the trend of polarization emerging in Egyptian politics as opposed to what seemed to be a pragmatic, inclusionary and participatory political bloc some weeks ago. See Khaled Dawoud, "Tahrir's countershow of force," *Al Ahram Weekly*, August 11–17 2011, accessed August 23, 2011, http://weekly.ahram.org.eg/2011/1060/fr1.htm.

34. Ibid.

35. Interview with an official from presidential candidate Dr El Baradei's team, Cairo, July 28, 2011.

36. Amounting to some 173 at present.

37. Interview with an official from presidential candidate Dr El Baradei's team, Cairo, July 28, 2011.

5

Palestine

Michael Schulz

This chapter will analyze how the EU's security thinking in the field of democracy and human rights has unfolded in relation to the Palestinian Authority (PA) in the so-called Palestinian self-rule areas in the West Bank and Gaza Strip. In order to do so this chaper will 1) address the role that the EU has played in promoting human rights and democracy in the Palestinian self-rule areas and the effectiveness of those policies; 2) assess the response of the EU to events and protests that were inspired by the Arab Spring throughout the Palestinian self-rule areas during this year; and 3) discuss the steps that European countries need to take in light of these developments. It will be argued that the EU overall framing of the Israeli-Palestinian Conflict (IPC) historically can be linked to its way of framing normative positions in relation to human rights and democratic principles. Also, when scrutinizing the EU implementation of its policies historically, they clash with these normative positions of the EU. A clear tension and contradiction exists between supporting the security needs of Israel and the PA on the one hand and espousing the democracy- and human rights-oriented needs of the Palestinians on the other. However, in the light of the events of the Arab Spring, the EU has somewhat shifted its strategies, possibly indicating new forms of action.

The Palestinian Case in the Light
of the Arab Spring in 2011

Since the various revolts in the Arab world, starting in October 2010 in Yemen and December 2010 in Tunisia, the Palestinians too have mobilized. However, the Palestinians are in a somewhat different position to the other Arab states. First, the Palestinian Authority (PA) is a self-rule authority and not a state (at best an embryonic state structure). Second, the PA has been split into two parts since 2007. The Fatah movement controls the West Bank PA with President Mahmoud Abbas in the frontline, while the Hamas government of Prime Minister Ismail Haniyeh controls the Gaza Strip PA. Third, the Oslo II Agreement, which divides the West Bank into three parts (area A in full control of PA, area B under joint Israeli and Palestinian control and area C under full Israeli control), places Palestinians under both *de jure* and *de facto* continued Israeli occupation. The Gaza Strip is isolated and under siege due to the Israeli boycott of the Hamas government. This boycott came after Hamas' election victory in 2006 when Hamas failed to meet the three conditions of the United States and the EU: to announce the prevention of armed struggle against Israeli occupation, to accept Israel's legitimate right to exist, and to accept the previous agreement the PLO signed with Israel. This contributed to harsh living conditions for the Palestinians and for *de facto* continued occupation, making basic human rights and democracy issues more complex.

On 15 March 2011, in a similar vein to other citizens' protests in the region, the Palestinian public started protesting against their two PA governments. In practice, their protest was directed more against Hamas' and Fatah's unwillingness to reconcile their differences after rivalry had led to their splitting in June 2007, with Hamas taking control of the Gaza Strip and Fatah of the West Bank. The Palestinian public felt increasingly upset by the dilemmas arising from the power division and accused both PAs of breaking human rights principles on a daily basis.

Demonstrations and hunger strikes occurred throughout every Palestinian city in the West Bank and the Gaza Strip. The protesters demanded, among other things, that all Palestinian political prisoners in Fatah and Hamas controlled areas be released. Also, that all political factions that joined forces within the PLO in the struggle against Israeli occupation, form a national government and announce new national and presidential elections. Further, they asked for a freeze in the negotiations with Israel until unity among the Palestinian faction had been reached. Finally, they requested that all Fatah and Hamas media campaigns against each other be instantly halted.

On 27 April 2011, after Egyptian mediation, the Reconciliation Agreement was officially announced and signed on May 4 between the two parties in Cairo. The key points Fatah and Hamas agreed upon were that "[t]he Legislative, Presidential, and the Palestinian National Council elections will be conducted at the same time exactly one year after the signing of the Palestinian National Reconciliation Agreement."[1]

Further, "[b]oth Fatah and Hamas agree to form a Palestinian government and to appoint the Prime Minister and Ministers in consensus between them."[2] Thus, most of the demands requested by the 15th March protest movement were taken into account by the agreement. However, since the initiative stemmed mainly from pressure from below, no real true reconciliation has taken place between the parties. Cognizant of this eventuality, the 15th March protest movement formed a coalition in May to protect the Reconciliation Agreement. To date, Hamas and Fatah have not installed a new government and it remains to be seen if they will hold elections before May 2012.

The goal of this chapter is to investigate what the EU has been doing since the protests started in March 2011, and how it has positioned itself in relation to the requests of the protesters. Also, on a broader level, in what way is the EU promoting human rights and democracy in the Palestinian self-rule areas?

EU on Human Rights and Democracy

Since the Treaty of Maastricht in 1992 the EU has considered human rights and democracy particularly worthy of attention, both internally as well as in its external relations. The framework of the European Neighbourhood Policy that was initiated in early 2002 aimed at ensuring that friendly neighbors would surround the EU's new members. The EU intended to actively promote human rights and democracy in neighborhood areas such as in Caucasia and the Mediterranean, thereby creating a stable neighbourhood area. The EU underlined that "[r]esolution of the Arab/Israeli conflict is a strategic priority for Europe."[3] The Barcelona Process launched in 1995 was intended to support and push forward the peace process between Israel and the Palestinians and to forge closer relations between the EU and its Mediterranean neighbors.[4]

EU Promotion of Human Rights and Democracy in Palestine

The normative position of the EU as a human rights and democracy promoter has had a somewhat varied history in the Palestinian case. In 1980 the then EC member states agreed to the Venice Declaration that stipulated a two-state solution to the Israeli-Palestinian conflict. A Palestinian state would be established beside Israel and would be democratic. With the Venice Declaration the nine EEC members stated "the right to existence and to security of all States in the region, including Israel, and justice for all the peoples, which implies the recognition of the legitimate rights of the Palestinian people . . . to exercise fully its right to self-determination."[5]

The EU's position was to go along with a two-state solution based on UN Security Council resolutions 242 and 338. All policies were henceforth based on the idea that a Palestinian state would be established in the future. Only then would democracy and human rights be a reality for the Palestinian people. The Oslo Accords of 1993 established a period of Palestinian self-rule in parts of the West Bank and the Gaza Strip. Hence, human rights and democracy issues became not merely issues linked to prevent Israeli violations against human rights in the occupied territories, but also how the new PA would link to democratic principles and follow the human rights in relation to its public constituencies. The EU was keen from the very beginning of the peace process to promote itself as a body which pushed for these principles.

The EU sees its overarching political security governance strategies in the ME peace process as entailing: 1. Political and economic relations, through association agreements and ENP Action Plans, with Israel, the PA, Lebanon, Jordan, and Egypt (and potentially also with Syria). 2. Regional dialogue forums, through the Euro-Mediterranean Partnership, whereby all parties to the conflict meet and discuss issues (not further specified). 3. Participation in the Quartet (EU, US, Russia and the UN), specifically supporting the Road Map towards a Palestinian state (UNSC resolution 1397), financial and human resources to the Office of the Quartet representative Tony Blair, and dialogue with third countries on the ME peace process (Catherine Ashton). 4. Consultations with all partners of the region (including the Arab League). 5. Regular issuing of policy statements by EU foreign ministers and the European Council.[6]

EU implementation of these overarching strategies in the ME peace process entails: 1. Being the main financial support to the Palestinian population (European Commission and Member States). 2. Creating regional peace, stability, and prosperity through humanitarian and emergency aid (through UNRWA and the PEGASE mechanism), state-building activities that empower the PA and complement PA plans, developing the penal and judiciary system and the police force through the EUPOL COPPS mission, and encouraging the Palestinian private sector. 3. Different kinds of assistance managed by EC Technical Assistance Office in Jerusalem. 4. Organizing customs and trade into the Palestinian territories and within the PA.[7] 5. Border assistance between Gaza and Egypt through the EUBAM Rafah mission. 6. Organizing dialogue between the European Commission, Israel, and the PA regarding policy on trade, transport, and energy. 7. Supporting different civil society projects ("people to people" projects).[8]

The EU invested heavily in strengthening Palestinian civil society, and in many respects, Palestinian civil society took upon itself the role of pushing for democratization of the PA. From

1994 to 2004 there were tense discussions between Palestinian civil society and the PA run by Yassir Arafat as to the form that Palestinian self-rule should take.

Regarding peace between Israel and Palestine specifically, the EU has a standpoint on the five final status issues, namely borders (in accordance with UNSC resolutions), settlements (illegal according to international law), Jerusalem (not stating the status of the city), refugees (supporting a just, viable, and agreed solution to the issue, but not stating how) and security (condemning all sorts of violence as undermining peace attempts and urging the Israeli government to act according to international law).[9]

The EU Response to Grassroots Protests

Since the revolutions began, during the so-called Arab Spring, the EU has been more focused on events taking place in the other Arab states (i.e., Egypt, Libya, Syria, and Tunisia, etc.) than on human rights and democracy issues in the Palestinian self-rule areas. Two documents produced in May, one by the European Council, linked to the reconciliation talks between Fatah and Hamas, and one by the European Commission called "A New Response to a Changing Neighbourhood," underline the EU's desire to "provide greater support to partners engaged in building deep democracy" which includes supporting free and fair elections, freedom of association, expression and assembly, a free press and media, rule of law, fighting corruption, security and law enforcement sector reform, and the establishment of democratic control over armed and security forces.[10]

The form of support is to establish partnership in each neighboring country and support civil society, establish a European Endowment for Democracy to help different actors of a country, promote media and internet development, and reinforce human rights dialogue.[11] The particular focus of the human rights dialogue will be gender equality.

While the above-mentioned forms of support refer to the entire region, the European Council came up with a more specific statement in reference to the peace process. It stated that "fundamental changes across the Arab world have made the need for progress on the Middle East peace process all the more urgent."[12] In relation to the Fatah-Hamas dialogue of May 2011, the EU indicated its support of the reconciliation efforts and stated that it "welcomes the agreement signed in Cairo on May 3." This position contrasts with that of US President Obama who, in his speech a few days earlier, had underlined that he was concerned that President Mahmoud Abbas was prepared to negotiate with an organization (Hamas) that the US government considered to be terrorist.

However, given the historical fact that the EU has constantly promoted the two-state solution and given legitimacy to the PLO and Fatah leaders in particular, the statement indicates a potential shift in the direction of a pragmatic and inclusive position towards Hamas. This small diplomatic shift is not merely an indication of the EU's position vis-à-vis the United States, but most likely a result of discussions that have been taking place in the EU since Hamas' election victory 2006 and subsequent boycott. Several countries are increasingly critical of the boycott, believing that it ruins any future chance of constructive dialogue with Hamas. It also places them in a spoiler position, making it harder to reach a compromise solution with Israel.

Despite different EU documents, as well as the EU official website, that employs critical language of Israel, accusing it of conducting unacceptable and counterproductive acts toward the Palestinian population, such as settlement construction and the closure of Gaza, it has in practice never abandoned its support for the Fatah-run PA. Historically, at the same time, the EU has continually expressed its understanding for Israeli security concerns and has condemned all manner of Palestinian violence against and among the Israeli population. This has caused the Palestinians to seriously question the EU's real intentions. Hence, it needs to be seen if the EU will act according to its declared intentions.

Alongside the extended family structure (*hamuleh*), civil society has become a safe system for many Palestinians who perceive the Palestinian Authority as corrupt and/or powerless. Civil society has taken care of many important sectors that a "nascent state" normally takes care of, such as health care, education, child care, human rights, etc. However, most civil society organizations are also linked to the various political factions in Palestinian society. The EU has supported many of these civil society organizations; some, particularly the Ramallah-, Bethlehem-, and Jerusalem-based organizations, have come to be seen by Palestinians as donor driven and corrupt, the tools of different factions and not independent civil society players. Donors tend not to include Islamic charity organizations in civil society but instead consider them a sector within Islamic political movements, supporting the weakest groups of society through that channel. At the same time, Islamic as well as secular civil society organizations have played an important role in highlighting democratization and human rights issues within the PA. This has led to increased criticism of the EU which is seen as one-sided in its support for Israeli security needs on the one hand, and in its support of the corrupt Fatah-dominated PA on the other.[13]

Several sectors within which the EU is active have also come in for criticism. For instance, the EU initiated and implemented reform within the security sector of the civil police. Its efforts to turn the West Bank Palestinian civil police into a disciplined and efficient police force met with some limited success, but had some unintended consequences.[14] Some security branches that do not follow rule of law principles and thus contravene human rights standards are supported by both the EU and the United States in their attempts to clamp down on Hamas. The idea that EU involvement indirectly supports Israeli security needs is hard to deny.

It is also hard to see how such a reform can succeed without the ending of the Israeli occupation, which is the root cause of the lack of human security. Despite the even lower levels of trust shown in the police and security forces of Hamas in the Gaza Strip, it must be asked whether Hamas' international isolation and boycott does not in fact further contribute to increasing human insecurity. The EU is part of this boycott.

The implementation of EU principles in the areas of law enforcement, democracy, and implementation of human rights have had a somewhat mixed and critical reception. Although the

EUPOL COPPS mission has generally been viewed positively, in that the public[15] shows increased trust in the police force, the reform leaves out those security branches that arrest Hamas supporters. Also, Hamas security forces are not part of the reform, thereby creating two separate police and security forces and dividing the two PAs still further.

Policy Implications for the EU

The EU's way of defining democracy and the human rights situation in relation to the overall Israeli-Palestinian conflict does not necessarily follow stringent EU governance strategy. The way the EU defines the conflict and perceives events influences which actors it chooses to support. Its one-sided support of the PLO/Fatah, has contributed to weaken democratization and human rights in the PA. Simultaneously, its harsh criticism and boycott of Hamas has, in the eyes of the Palestinians, placed the EU on the same side as Israel and the United States, thereby compromising its impartial status. When the Fatah-run PA tried to bring the statehood issue to the UN Security Council in September 2011, the EU followed the line that it would not support the announcement of a Palestinian state inside the 1949 armistice lines (the West Bank and the Gaza Strip).

The de facto EU policy of turning a blind eye to the many human rights abuses directed towards Palestinian groups opposed to Fatah in the West Bank, as well as Israel's human rights abuses when hunting down Hamas activists, further harms the EU's standing among the Palestinians.

The EU needs to reconsider its strategy and find a way of becoming more impartial. EU intervention should be seen by the public as distinct from other actors' interventions. That is not to say that no interventions should be coordinated multilaterally. However, if multilateral interventions risk creating a perception of the EU as partial and foment distrust, it is prudent for the EU to steer away from direct involvement. The EU should rather work to convince the partners of the EU Roadmap, and the parties to the conflict, for a two-state solution. It should push human rights and democracy principles on the ground, without compromising them for fear of being accused of not supporting Israeli security concerns, or of weakening the Fatah PA in the West Bank.

Notes

1. The Fatah-Hamas Reconciliation Agreement, 27th April 2011. Accessed November 5, 2011, http://www.palestinemonitor.org/spip/spip.php?article1787.

2. Ibid.

3. European Security Strategy, "A Secure Europe in a Better World," accessed on November 4, 2011, http://www.consilium.europa.eu/uedocs/cmsUpload/78367.pdf. See also Melhia Benli Al-tunisik, "EU foreign Policy and the Israeli-Palestinian conflict: How much of an Actor?," *European Security* 17 no. 1, (2008): 105–21.

4. Nathalie Tocci, "Conflict Resolution in the Neighbourhood: Comparing EU Involvement in Turkey's Kurdish Question and in the Israeli-Palestinian Conflict," in *Mediterranean Politics* 10 no. 2 (2005): 125–46. See also, Ricardo Gomez, *Negotiating the Euro-Mediterranean Partnership. Strategic Action in EU Foreign Policy?* (Aldershot: Ashgate, 2003).

5. See Sharon Pardo and Joel Peters, *Israel and the European Union: A Documentary History* (Lanham, MD: Lexington Books, 2011).

6. European Union External Action, "EU Political Support for the Middle East Peace Process," accessed November 4, 2011, http://eeas.europa.eu/mepp/political/political_en.htmhttp://eeas.europa.eu/mepp/political/political_en.htm.

7. Council Joint Action 2005/797/CFSP of November 14, 2005 on the European Union Police Mission for the Palestinian Territories, OJ L 300, 17.11.2005, Article 2, item 1: 66. See also Council Joint Action 2005/889/CFSP of December 12, 2005 on establishing a European Union Border Assistance Mission for the Rafah Crossing Point (EU BAM Rafah), OJ L 327 14.12.2005, p. 28, Article 2.b., accessed November 4, 2011, http://www.eubam-rafah.eu/portal/en/node/18.

8. European Union External Action, "EU Practical and Financial Support for the Middle East Peace Process," accessed November 4, 2011, http://eeas.europa.eu/mepp/practical/practical_en.htmhttp://eeas.europa.eu/mepp/practical/practical_en.htm.

9. European Union External Action, "EU Positions on the Middle East Process," accessed November 4, 2011, http://eeas.europa.eu/mepp/eu-positions/eu_positions_en.htm

10. "A New Response to a Changing Neighbourhood: A Review of the European Neighbourhood Policy," EU Joint communication by the High Representative of the Union for Foreign Affairs and Security Policy and the European Commission, Brussels, 25 May, 2011: 2. Accessed November 4, 2011, http:// ec.europa.eu/world/enp/pdf/com_11_303_en.pdf.

11. Ibid.

12. Council of the European Union, Council Conclusions on Middle East Peace Process, 3091st Foreign Affairs Council meeting, Brussels, 23 May, 2011. Accessed November 4, 2011, http://www.consilium.europa.eu/uedocs/cms_Data/docs/.../122165.pdf.

13. Michael Schulz, "The European Union as Third Party in the Israeli-Palestinian Conflict" in *War and Peace in Transition: Changing Roles and Practices of External Actors*, eds. Karin Aggestam and Annika Björkdahl (Lund: Nordic Academic Press, 2009), 72–89. Also Nathalie Tocci, *The EU and Conflict Resolution: Promoting Peace in the Backyard* (London and New York: Routledge, 2007). See also Roland Friedrich and Arnold Luethold, "And they Came in and Took Possession of Reforms: Ownership and Palestinian SSR," in *Local Ownership and Security Sector Reform* (Geneva: Centre for the Democratic Control of Armed Forces (DCAF)) 2008: 191–213.

14. Yezid Sayigh, "Fixing Broken Windows": Security Sector Reform in Palestine, Lebanon, and Yemen," *Carnegie Papers* No. 17, 2009, accessed November 4, 2011, http://carnegieendowment.org/2009/10/27/fixing-broken-windows-security-sector-reform-in-palestine-lebanon-and-yemen/3gl. Also Yezid Sayigh, "Inducing a Failed State in Palestine," *Survival* 49, 3 (2007): 7–39.

15. Michael Schulz, "Whose Security in Palestine? EU Intervention's Impact on Security Sector Reform in Palestine," *Development Dialogue*, Special issue on *Intervention as the New Security Order: Towards Global Disaster Management*, (forthcoming 2012). See also, Michael Schulz, "Palestinian Public Willingness to Compromise: Torn Between Hope and Violence," *Journal of Security Dialogues*, 2, 1 (2011): 117–40.

6

Israel

Joel Peters

The role of the European Union in the promotion of civil society and human rights in Israel differs significantly from the challenges it faces when addressing the same issue with other countries in the Mediterranean and Middle East region. The starting point in the discussions between Israel and the EU on this question is different in two respects. First Israel and the European Union have developed an extensive and ever-increasing network of political, economic, and cultural ties. The balance sheet in terms of personal and civil society connections, the numerous scientific cooperative ventures in the field of research and development, and the economic content of Israeli-EU relations are positive and solid. More critically, the EU regards Israel, in sharp contrast to all other countries in the region, as "a democratic state with associated political rights, respect for the rule of law and a flourishing civil society."[1] The EU 2004 Country Report on Israel details the range of international human rights and labor conventions to which Israel is a signatory, and points to domestic legislation in a number of areas such as free and open elections, freedom of speech and freedom of the press, workers rights, equal opportunities, and women's representation in the public sphere and judicial system, in all of which Israel scores highly. The Report also praises Israeli civil society for its diversity and its activism in the sphere of social, cultural, and human rights and makes special mention of the high regard in which human rights organizations are held by the international community, not only for their advocacy, but also for the accuracy with which they report human rights abuses.

That is not to say that the question of human rights and support for civil society organizations has never been a point of friction in Israeli-European relations. European civil society perceptions of Israel and Israeli society in this respect are not always favorable. As with other Mediterranean and Middle Eastern states, the EU's relations with Israel are governed by a number of policy instruments, most specifically the 1995 EU-Israel Association Agreement and the 2004 European Neighborhood EU/Israel Action Plan. As in all Association Agreements, the EU-Israel Association Agreement includes the "essential element" clause highlighting the importance of human rights in governing the development of future relations. Article 2 of the agreement states that: "relations between the parties, as well as all the provisions of the agreement itself, shall be based on respect for human rights and democratic principles, which guides their internal and international policy and constitutes an essential element of this agreement." The new Action Plan builds on this platform noting that special attention will be given to the common values of "respect for human rights and fundamental freedoms, democracy, the rule of law, good governance and international law" and that "the degree of commitment to those values will determine the level of ambition and the pace of progress of the future EU-Israel relationship."[2]

This chapter will address how the issue of human rights and Europe's promotion of human rights within Israel has impacted on Israeli-European relations and how discussion of this question will determine the future of those ties. The chapter will focus on three areas. First, it will address growing European concerns over Israeli violations of Palestinian human rights in the Occupied Territories and discuss how in recent years the issue of human security has entered into European statements and discourse on the Israeli-Palestinian conflict. Second, it will show how the European Union has sought to open up a dialogue with

Israel over the question of the civil and economic rights of its Palestinian Arab citizens and other minority groups. The final section will address how European support for Israeli human rights organizations, and recent Israeli legislation aimed at undermining and delegitimizing the work of those organizations, has emerged as a new source of friction between Israel and Europe.

Europe, Human Rights, and the Israeli-Palestinian Conflict

Without question, it is the differences over the Israeli-Palestinian conflict and the legal status of the West Bank, Gaza, and East Jerusalem that have most soured Israeli-European relations over the past thirty-five years. In contrast to Israel, the European Union has long considered the Fourth Geneva Convention concerning the protection of populations against the consequences of war and their protection in occupied territories as applicable to Israel's actions in the West Bank, Gaza, and East Jerusalem. Accordingly, the EU has condemned the appropriation of land and the construction of Israeli settlements as illegal under international law. European states have never recognized Israel's annexation of East Jerusalem in 1967 and have consistently warned Israel against taking unilateral measures which would alter the character of the city.

Yet the condition of Palestinian human rights in the Occupied Territories rarely featured in European discourse and policies in the years prior to the signing of the Oslo Accords in 1993, nor during the Oslo peace process itself. Although the European Union remained critical of Israeli settlement building, road closures and Israel's actions in East Jerusalem, it saw those actions primarily as obstacles to the achievement of peace rather than human rights concerns. For Europe, Palestinian rights would be secured by ending Israel's occupation and through the achievement of national self-determination and eventual statehood (see chapter by Schulz in this volume). It was only after the collapse of the Oslo process at the end of 2000 and the outbreak of the al-Aqsa Intifada that the EU introduced a human rights framing into its discourse on the Israeli-Palestinian conflict. Since that point European statements on the Israeli-Palestinian conflict have increasingly focused on the importance of human security, signaling its growing unease at the extent of Israeli human rights violations in the Occupied Territories, such as the policy of targeted assassinations, the obstruction of freedom of movement for Palestinians, the economic blockade of Gaza, and what Europeans see as Israel's (over)reliance on military measures to ensure its security.

Three reasons can be put forward for the introduction of a human rights framing into European positioning on the Israeli-Palestinian conflict. First, Israel's use of overwhelming military force to put down the Palestinian uprising and counter the wave of suicide attacks drew widespread criticism in European circles. In the first months of the al-Aqsa Intifada, the IDF fired one million rounds of ammunition—700,000 in the West Bank and 300,000 in Gaza and from 29 September to late October 2000, 118 Palestinians were killed, including 33 under the age of 18. While the European Union condemned Palestinian attacks on Israeli citizens, they castigated Israel for its harsh measures, its policy of targeted assassinations, the destruction of Palestinian infrastructure (much of which had been financed by the EU), and what they saw as the disproportionate use of military force by Israel: "Israel's security concerns are legitimate, but they must be addressed with full respect for human rights and within the framework of the rule of law. The EU urges Israel to put an immediate end to activities that are inconsistent with international humanitarian law and human rights, such as extra-judicial killings, to abstain from all acts of collective punishment such as demolition of Palestinian homes, to lift closures and curfews and to abstain from deportations of family members. The EU firmly believes that there can be no justification for military actions directed indiscriminately against civilian neighborhoods."[3] European Commissioner Chris Patten reflected the mood within European civil society, warning Israel that its military operations were causing colossal damage to its reputation as a democracy. He went on to accuse Israel of trampling over "the rule of law, over the Geneva conventions, over what are generally regarded as [the] acceptable norms of behavior."[4] The EU has continued to issue similar statements in response to Israel's military actions over the past decade, most notably following Israel's military (re)invasion of Gaza in December 2008.

Second, the almost daily images of Israel's military actions and the destruction of Palestinian infrastructure in the media, and now also the electronic media, led to a noticeable shift in the engagement and attitudes within European civil society on the conflict and to a subsequent weakening of Israel's global image. Many Europeans began to openly express doubts as to whether Israel was truly interested in peace. In November 2003, for example, an EU-commissioned survey found that 59 percent of Europeans saw Israel as posing "the greatest threat to world peace."[5] Nearly 35 percent of Europeans polled believed that the Israeli army intentionally targeted Palestinian civilians.[6] The tide of public anger against Israel led to a shift in Europe's approach. As in all spheres of public life, those European NGOs working in the Occupied Territories began to play an increasingly influential role in determining the public discourse and the policy preferences of the European governments on the Israeli-Palestinian conflict.

Finally, following the collapse of the peace process there was acknowledgement of the need to address questions of human security more directly, matched by a recognition that this aspect of peace building had been overlooked during the Oslo process. This reflected the awareness within European policy circles of the importance of human security as an integral element of European foreign policy (see chapter by Fioramonti in this volume). The 2003 European Security Strategy (ESS) described the post Cold War environment as "one of increasingly open borders in which the internal and external aspects of security are indissolubly linked." It also pointed to the fundamental interconnectedness of security, human rights, and democracy and considered the protection of human rights and democracy a fundamental ingredient of a peaceful and secure international order. "The best protection for our security is a world of well-governed democratic states. Spreading good governance, supporting social and political reforms, dealing with corruption and abuse of power, establishing the rule of law, and protecting human rights are the best means of strengthening the international order."[7]

Israel's (over)reliance on military measures to secure its defense was viewed in Europe as disproportionate and was seen not only as being in contravention of international law and international humanitarian law, but also as a contributory factor in the rising tensions in the region. For many Europeans, Israel needs to be more cognizant of the human aspects of security, such as the respect for human rights, economic welfare, and development, and not just its military aspects. European reactions and criticism of Israeli policies such as the building of the separation barrier, the restriction of movement in the West Bank, the economic blockade of Gaza during the past five years, and its actions in Jerusalem have increasingly drawn attention to the human costs and suffering inflicted on the Palestinian population and the worsening humanitarian conditions in the West Bank and Gaza.

The European Union has limited its response to declaratory diplomacy, a commonly used European instrument in response to problems of human rights in third countries, by increasingly highlighting the issue of human rights in its statements on the Israeli-Palestinian conflict. In principle, the EU could utilize article 2 and article 79 of the 1995 Association Agreement as instruments of conditionality and sanction Israel for its actions. However, the EU has been unwilling to go down this route, believing that dialogue with Israel is preferable. Voices from various sectors to call Israel to account for its human rights record (and the ongoing construction of settlements in the West Bank) have not garnered (nor are they likely to) any significant support within European capitals. Instead Europe has focused its efforts on funding Israeli human rights organizations which have championed the cause of human rights in the Occupied Territories and have served as a watchdog on Israeli policies. The funding of those organizations by the European governments and the European Union has attracted growing criticism in Israel (see below).

The EU and Israel's Palestinian Arab Minority

The European Commission has over the years flagged its concerns over Israel's discriminatory policies towards its Arab citizens. But it was not until the adoption of the EU/Israel Action Plan in 2004 that this concern became an item for discussion between the two sides. In the Action Plan's section on "political dialogue and cooperation" Israel and the EU committed themselves to the promotion of "their shared values of democracy, rule of law . . . respect for human rights . . . international humanitarian law . . . [to] promote and protect rights of minorities, including enhancing political, economic, social and cultural opportunities for all citizens and lawful residents . . . and monitoring of policies from the perspective of gender equality." The Action Plan further states, "the degree of commitment to these values will determine the level of ambition and the pace of progress of the future EU-Israel relationship" though it fails to offer any insight how this "degree of commitment" will be measured and what costs or sanctions (if any) might be imposed due to lack of progress in this area or any violations of human rights by Israel.[8] The Action Plan is high in principles but low on details for future action. It suggests blandly "the possibility" of Israel exploring the idea of "joining the optional protocols related to international conventions on human rights," without specifying which human conventions or demanding any real commitment from Israel.[9] Nor does it propose any joint programs or suggest ways in which the rights of Israel's Palestinian citizens might be advanced.

In its 2004 Country Report on Israel the EU was strongly critical of Israel over its introduction the previous year of an amendment to the law on Israeli citizenship by which the granting of citizenship or residency rights to Palestinians from the Occupied Territories who were married to Israeli citizens would now be prohibited. The amendment to the citizenship law drew criticism not only from the international community, but also from Israeli human rights organizations which protested the negative impact it would have on the rights of Israel's Palestinian citizens. Yet the EU/Israel Action Plan, which drew heavily on the 2004

Country Report, was surprisingly silent on this amendment to the citizenship law.[10]

As a result of the Action Plan, Israel and the EU created an informal working group to discuss the question of human rights. Their four hour meeting once a year is, however, hardly sufficient for an in-depth sustained dialogue on the issues facing Israel's Palestinian citizens and other human rights concerns. The meetings are attended by low-level officials who convene alongside a working group on international organizations. Neither Israel (nor the European Union) has developed any consultative mechanisms to engage civil society organizations prior to or after the meetings. The European Union has sought repeatedly to upgrade this informal working group to the level of a standing subcommittee on human rights, but so far Israel has denied this request.

This issue, however, remains a low priority for the European Union in its relations with Israel whom it has not pressed to develop this dialogue. Instead, the European Commission has confined itself to issuing bland comments each year on the lack of progress in this area. The 2008 Progress Report on the Implementation of the European Neighbourhood Policy merely states, "progress with regard to the promotion of democracy, rule of law and respect for human rights and international humanitarian law was limited. . . . Overall, the promotion and protection of the Israeli Arab minority remained unsatisfactory during the reporting period."[11]

Europe has focused its efforts on supporting civil society initiatives such as the development of human rights programs at university and college level, and providing financial support for human rights campaigns and civil society organizations such as: Adalah (The Legal Center for Arab Minority Rights in Israel), Mossawa (The Advocacy Center for Arab Citizens in Israel), Sikkuy (The Association for the Advancement of Civic Equality in Israel), and Shatil (The New Israel Fund's Empowerment and Training Center for Social Change Organizations in Israel).[12] Given the overall health and size of its economy (Israel has a larger GDP per capita than many EU member states), Israel is not eligible for development assistance from the EU. The funding for human rights organizations in Israel (through the European Instrument for Democracy and Human Rights, EIDHR) amounts to €1.2 million (Euro) per year and has developed into a controversial new point of tension between Israel and the EU under the current Israeli government.

The EU, Human Rights, and the Netanyahu Government

In recent years a number of right-wing groups in Israel, most notably Im Tirtzu and NGO Monitor, have launched high-profile campaigns with the aim of delegitimizing the activities of Israeli civil society and human rights organizations, especially those that advocate the rights of Arab citizens of Israel and/or address the question of Israeli violations of human rights in the Occupied Territories. Those attacks gained increasing force after the publication of the Goldstone Report in September 2009. In a similar vein, some government representatives have suggested that human rights organizations now pose a strategic threat for Israel, with Israeli Foreign Minister Avigdor Lieberman even accusing them of acting as accomplices to terrorism. The growing hostility to the work of civil society groups has led to a spate of anti-democratic bills presented to the Israeli Knesset over the past two years. This legislation either infringes the rights of Israeli citizens, most notably the rights of minority groups, or is aimed at undercutting the activities of various civil society organizations, especially those whose opinions are viewed unfavorably by the current political majority in Israel. The most notable of these bills are:

- an amendment to the 1952 Citizenship Law by which naturalized citizens would now have to swear allegiance to the State of Israel "as a Jewish democratic state";
- "the Nakba Bill"—that penalizes any organization receiving public funding that marks Israel's day of independence as a day of mourning or denies that Israel is a Jewish democratic state;

- the Anti-Boycott Law—that makes any activities that advocate any kind of boycott of Israeli organizations, individuals, or goods a criminal offense. The prime purpose of this bill was counter calls for a boycott of goods produced in Israeli settlements in the West Bank;
- the NGO Funding Bill—by which civil groups would be required to state the source of funding for their advocacy campaign should they receive funding from foreign political entities (i.e., foreign governments).[13]

Two separate bills calling for the setting up of a parliamentary committee of inquiry to investigate the financing of various NGOs were presented to the Knesset plenum in July 2011 but failed to gain sufficient support. Israel's prime minister Binyamin Netanyahu had initially favored the creation of those committees, but withdrew his support at the last minute in light of rising public and international opposition to the measure.

Hostility towards human rights NGOs was reflected in the decision of several members of the Israeli Knesset to host a conference at the end of 2009 that addressed the funding of the political activities of Israeli NGOs by foreign governments, and in particular highlighted the role of European governments' support for those organizations. The European Union has been highly critical of this new legislation. In a statement issued on 22 February 2011 following the tenth meeting of the EU-Israel Association Council, the EU denounced the passing of the "loyalty oath" and the "Nakba Bill" for having "a strong alienating effect on the Israeli Arab community." The statement also expressed European concern that those bills "could, inter alia, be used to entrench segregation between Jewish and Arab citizens of Israel."[14] The EU was equally critical of the passing of the anti-boycott law in July 2011. In a carefully crafted statement, the EU stressed that it was not advocating the use of boycotts but, nonetheless, had strong reservations "about the effect that this legislation may have on the freedom of Israeli citizens to express non-violent political opinions"[15] and that it would continue its dialogue with the Israeli government over this issue.

European governments have looked upon the "NGO Funding Bill" with particular consternation, seeing it, and with good cause, as directed against European support of Israeli human rights organizations. Ostensibly this legislation is concerned with creating greater transparency, but the impetus behind the bill is a palpable anti-European agenda. Attacks on various civil society organizations such as the New Israel Fund, Mossawa, and Adalah have been accompanied by criticism of European support for those organizations. At the 2009 Knesset conference on NGO funding, European countries and the EU were singled out for special attention. In his speech to that conference, Gerald Steinberg, the founder and President of NGO Monitor, accused European governments of deliberately setting out to manipulate the political process in Israel. For Steinberg the scale of European support was unprecedented in relations between democratic countries: "Behind the façade of civil society the EU and its member states are giving public funds to a small number of opposition groups . . . with anonymous European officials in charge of NGO allocations seeking to exploit a minority group of Israelis to impose EU favored policies on the wider Israel public." Addressing members of the European Parliament Steinberg charged that the political advocacy organizations that received European funding were leading "the campaign embodying [a] 'third generation' of warfare against Israel . . . . with the stated goal of ending Jewish national self-determination [by] using the façade of human rights."[16]

This issue has also caught the attention of members of the European Parliament. To the dismay of Israel, the human rights subcommittee of the Parliament convened a special session in June 2010 to address the situation of NGOs and civil society in Israel. The issue was then debated at the full parliamentary session in September. At that session EU Commissioner for Enlargement Stefan Füle informed the Parliament that Brussels held serious reservations about the bill, and that European concerns over the legislation had been raised on several occasions with the Israeli government. Füle noted that although some of the most controversial aspects of the bill had been dropped, the demand for transparency from the NGOs still remained too demanding and discriminated against those organizations reliant on public funds, notably those from the EU.[17]

Paradoxically the attacks on Israeli human rights organizations have served to focus European attention on the human security dimension of the Israeli-Palestinian conflict and on Israeli abuses of Palestinian human rights. Take for example the case of Abdallah Abu Rahmah, a leader of the non-violent protests against the separation barrier in the village of Bil'in in the West Bank. Abu Rahmah was arrested in December 2009 and was initially sentenced to twelve months imprisonment for incitement and organizing illegal demonstrations following an eight month trial in an Israeli military court. In January 2011, the court extended his sentence by a further three months. The European Union has highlighted Abu Rahmah's struggle and his imprisonment by Israel. In a strong show of solidarity, representatives from the EU delegation in Jerusalem attended all the court hearings and representatives from seven European countries were also present at the time of his sentencing. Catherine Ashton, the EU's high representative for foreign policy, denounced the decision to extend Abu Rahmah's sentence as deplorable, designed solely to intimidate him and deter other Palestinians "from exercising their legitimate right to protest against the existence of the separation barrier in a non-violent manner." Describing Abu Rahmah as a "human rights defender" Ashton reaffirmed Europe's support for the right of Palestinians to engage in peaceful demonstrations and reminded Israel in no uncertain terms that the EU considered the building of the separation barrier on Palestinian land as illegal. Not surprisingly, Israel took Ashton's comments as unwarranted interference in the judicial proceedings of another country. In a statement issued at the conclusion of the tenth meeting of the EU-Israel Association Council, the EU returned to the Abu Rahmah case, noting that its support for "human rights defenders was a long established element of the European Union's human rights external relations policy" and that it considered Israeli and Palestinian human rights activists as playing a crucial role in the promotion of the values of democracy, peace, and human rights."[18]

Conclusion—The Impact of the Arab Spring

The issue of human rights has not been a central feature of or an impediment to the development of Israeli-European relations. Despite growing European criticism of Israel's human rights violations in the Occupied Territories, its concerns over the civil and economic rights of Israel's Palestinian citizens, and its censure of Israel for recent legislation aimed at undercutting human rights NGOs, Israel and Europe have developed an intensive network of economic, political, and cultural ties. The balance sheet of Israeli-European relations remains strong and positive.

As discussed in this chapter, the issue of Israeli human rights violations and the living conditions of the Palestinians in the West Bank and Gaza has begun to receive more attention in European policy circles and entered European discourse on the peace process. This has been driven by a newfound awareness of the importance of human security (and an understanding that this aspect of peace building was ignored during the Oslo years) combined with the growing influence of European human rights NGOs in advocating this issue, and drawing attention to the humanitarian conditions of Palestinians in the West Bank and Gaza.

European criticism of Israel for its reliance on military measures to counter the threat of Palestinian terrorism and launching attacks from Gaza, and in particular the cost inflicted on the daily lives of Palestinians, is a major and ever-growing source of friction between Israel and Europe. Israel sees Europe's focus on human security issues and adherence to international humanitarian law as hollow and a reflection of Europe's lack of political will and capacity to counter this threat. Israel has accused Europeans of being indifferent to its security and failing to acknowledge the policy dilemmas it faces when trying to protect its citizens, especially against acts of terrorism. Above all, Israel accuses Europe of hypocrisy and failing to apply the same standards in the areas of human rights, good governance, and the rule of law to its dealings with the Arab world.

The focus on human security has been accompanied by calls within European civil society (and in some sectors of Israeli civil society) for Europe to adopt a more "rights-based" approach to the peace process and a more forceful response to Israel's human rights violations in the Occupied Territories and to its treatment of Palestinians. They argue that European leaders are not only failing the Palestinians, but also betraying Europe's own principles.[19] Calls for sanctions on Israel and increased conditionality as a result of its poor human rights record have not garnered much support within European capitals. The European Union considers the violation of Palestinian human rights and their declining humanitarian conditions a consequence of the political deadlock and ongoing Israeli occupation, rather than the source of Palestinian grievance. Through its membership of the Quartet the EU has sought ways to resume negotiations leading to the establishment of a Palestinian state.

Mention of the Israeli-Palestinian conflict in the Arab Spring has been conspicuous by its absence, featuring little in demonstrations across the wider Middle East. It is unclear how the events in the Middle East will unfold, but the peoples and new governments of the Middle East are likely to turn their attention back to the Israeli-Palestinian conflict and demand justice for the Palestinians. The new governments will be watching and judging the actions and policies of the European Union (as well as other international actors) with respect to Israeli policies in the West Bank and Gaza. The international community responded to the events of the past year with renewed efforts to bring Israel and the Palestinians back to negotiating. But given the domestic constraints facing both Israel and Palestinians, the unresolved question of Palestinian reconciliation and national unity, the predominance of the 2012 American presidential elections, and Europe's preoccupation with the Euro crisis, the prospects for any significant progress for a resolution of the Israeli-Palestinian conflict over the next eighteen months are low.

Given these trends, greater emphasis will be placed in the next eighteen months on socio-economic and humanitarian conditions in the West Bank and Gaza. There will be growing calls from the peoples of the region, and from within European civil society, for the European Union to translate its rhetoric on human security into practice. It will be tasked with bringing Israel to account for its practices in the West Bank and for the economic and political blockade of Gaza while increasing its financial and moral support for Palestinian and Israeli human rights NGOs. As a consequence the question of human rights is likely to assume a more prominent place on the Israel-European agenda and threatens to become a significant point of departure in the future development and direction of that relationship.

Notes

1. Commission of the European Communities, 2004. *European Neighbourhood Policy: Country Report, Israel*, 12 May 2004. *Brussels: Com (204) 373 final*. Accessed November 4, 2011, http://ec.europa.eu/world/enp/.../country/israel_enp_country_report_2004_en.pdf.

2. Those documents can be found in Sharon Pardo and Joel Peters, *Israel and the European Union: A Documentary History* (Lanham, MD: Lexington Books, 2011).

3. European Union, *Declaration of the European Union: Third Meeting of the Association Council EU-Israel*, 21 October 2002. Accessed November 4, 2011, http://www.consilium.europa.eu/ueDocs/cms_Data/docs/pressData/en/er/72832.pdf.

4. Ian Black, Ewan MacAskill, and Nocholas Watt, "Israel Faces Rage Over 'Massacre'," *The Guardian*, 17 April 2002.

5. Flash Eurobarometer, *Iraq and Peace in the World—Full Report 151, European Commission* 2003, accessed July 2009, http://www.mafhoum.com/press6/167P52.pdf.

6. Suzanne Gershowitz and Emanuele Ottolenghi, "Europe's Problem with Ariel Sharon," *Middle East Quarterly* 2005, accessed July 29, 2009, http://www.meforum.org/743/europes-problem-with-ariel-sharon.

7. European Security Strategy, *A Secure Europe in a Better World*, 2003. Accessed October, 15 2011, http://www.consilium.europa.eu/uedocs/cmsUpload/78367.pdf.

8. EU-Israel Association Council, 2004. *EU/Israel Action Plan*. Accessed November 4, 2011, http://ec.europa.eu/world/enp/pdf/action_plans/israel_enp_ap_final_en.pdf.

9. Israel has not ratified the two Optional Protocols to the International Convention on Civil and Political Rights, the Optional Protocol to the Convention on the Elimination of all Forms of Discrimination Against Women, and the Optional Protocol to the Convention Against Torture.

10. Raffaella Del Sarto, "Wording and Meaning(s): EU-Israeli Political Cooperation according to the ENP Action Plan" *Mediterranean Politics* 11, 1 (2007): 62.

11. European Commission, 2008. *Progress Report on the Implementation of the European Neighbourhood Policy, Israel*, 394, 3 April 2008, SEC(2008), accessed November 4, 2011, http://ec.europa.eu/world/enp/documents_en.htm#3.

12. For a full list of these projects see website of the delegation of the European Union to Israel. Accessed November 4, 2011, http://www.eeas.europa.eu/delegations/israel/projects/list_of_projects/projects_en.htm.

13. For details of those bills and other legislation see the Association of Civil Rights in Israel (ACRI) *Knesset Roundup*, accessed November 4, 2011, http://www.acri.org.il/en/?tag=knesset-roundup.

14. European Union, *Statement of the European Union: Tenth Meeting of the EU-Israel Association Council Statement of the European Union*, 22 February 2011. Accessed November 4, 2011, http://eeas.europa.eu/delegations/israel/press.../20110222_01_en.htm.

15. See *"European Union expresses concern over Israel's boycott law"* Ha'aretz, 13 July, 2001. Available at: http://www.haaretz.com/news/diplomacy-defense/european-union-expresses-concern-over-israel-s-boycott-law-1.373076. Accessed January 12, 2012.

16. Gerald M. Steinberg, *Europe's Hidden Hand: EU Funding for Political NGOs in the Arab Israeli Conflict: Analyzing Processes and Impact*, NGO Monitor Monograph Series 2. 2008. Accessed November 4, 2011, http://www.ngo-monitor.org/article/ngo_monitor_releases_groundbreaking_report_on_eu_funding_of_ngos. In January 2010, NGO Monitor filed a lawsuit against the European Commission at the European Court of Justice in order to obtain vital information related to EC funding of non-governmental organizations.

17. *EUObserver, EU warns Israel over anti-NGO bill*, 9 September 2010, accessed November 4, 2011, http://euobserver.com/24/30765.

18. European Union, *Statement of the European Union: Tenth Meeting of the EU-Israel Association Council Statement of the European Union*, 22 February 2011. Accessed November 4, 2011, http://eeas.europa.eu/delegations/israel/press.../20110222_01_en.htm.

19. Euro-Mediterranean Human Rights Network, 2011. *The EU and the Palestinian Arab Minority in Israel*. Accessed November 4, 2011, http://www.euromedrights.org/en/publications-en/emhrn-publications/emhrn-puplications/9132.html.

7

Lebanon and Syria

Carin Berg

The European Union (EU) policy reads that any country which has concluded agreements with the Union must respect human rights and democratic principles. In case a country violates these principles, the EU can use restrictive measures. The governments of Syria and Lebanon, despite being signatories to many international human rights accords, repeatedly infringe human rights and ignore democratic principles. Nevertheless, the EU has rarely employed punitive measures against the two countries. Syria's political and governmental procedures need a total overhaul in order for democracy and transparency to become rooted in the country. Lebanon, more advanced in the democratization process, needs support and maintenance.

This essay addresses the role the EU has played in promoting human rights and democracy in Lebanon and Syria and why it has or has not been effective in accomplishing its goals. It also assesses the role played by the EU following the Arab Spring in the areas of human rights and democracy promotion.

The histories of Lebanon and Syria are linked. On 14 March 2005 a large demonstration took place in Lebanon calling for the withdrawal of Syrian troops after almost thirty years presence. Civil society was requesting "a solid democratic framework allowing for genuine public participation and political representation."[1] When Syrian troops eventually withdrew and demands were voiced for elections and political change, the EU inevitably intervened in support of the democratization process.

In 1995, together with the EU member states, Lebanon and Syria launched the European-Mediterranean Partnership Initiative (EMP), also known as the Barcelona Process. It was through this initiative that specific guidelines for EU support for democracy and human rights were set out. In this chapter I will discuss why and how EU policy towards Lebanon and Syria has changed during 2011.

EU as a Human Rights and Democracy Promoter in Lebanon and Syria

EU and Lebanon

France's historical role has permeated EU relations with Syria and Lebanon. As a consequence of World War I when the Ottoman Empire was dissolved, France was assigned the mandate of modern Syria, which included Lebanon. The mandate lasted from 1923–1946, when both countries eventually became independent. The main aim for the French was to create a safe Christian/Maronite Lebanon under French protection which, not surprisingly, was rejected by the Muslim population which proposed re-unification with Syria.[2] France's original plan was, as we know today, not put into practice, but France has nonetheless taken the lead in relations with Lebanon, in the political, economic and cultural spheres.

On the political level, France has taken the lead in Lebanon's reconstruction, specifically after the Lebanese civil war which ended in 1990 and after the war with Israel in 2006. On the economic level, France (and Britain) had financial interests in Lebanon already during the colonial period when France monopolized the silk trade and sought to control Lebanese ports, roads and railways. Today, France serves as a very important European trade partner for both Syria and Lebanon.[3]

Joint EU relations with Lebanon and Syria began in 1977 with the Economic, Technical and Financial Cooperation Agreement with the Economic European Community (EEC), an agreement which still serves as the legal platform for cooperation between the three entities. The Cooperation Agreement includes the Association Agreement (AA), aimed at political change, democratic reform and human rights. In Lebanon the AA resulted in a complete agreement in 2002, but it is still awaiting full ratification by all EU member countries and thus has little effect, either in Lebanon or Syria.

The almost thirty-year Syrian occupation of Lebanon (1976–2005) has been a major obstacle to stability and democracy in the two countries, and a main issue for European policy. For example, many human rights violations in Syria were directly related to the Lebanese occupation when Syrian forces tortured and imprisoned Lebanese and Palestinian refugees on a daily basis. In the meantime, France expressed its support for reforms in Lebanon through the "Middle East and North Africa Initiative," which involved strengthening freedom and democracy. The EU, on its part, remained relatively silent on the matter.[4]

In Lebanon political transparency is greater than in Syria, but Lebanon is still permeated with internal tension in the aftermath of occupation (Israel and Syria). It is dealing with political divisions, minorities' issues, the Palestinian refugee question and regional concerns like relations between Hezbollah, Syria and Iran, etc. The Israeli occupation of southern Lebanon in 1982 was directly related to the Palestinian Liberation Organization (PLO), and therefore indirectly to the large Palestinian refugee mass which fled to Lebanon as a consequence of the Arab-Israeli conflict in 1948. The PLO was expelled from Jordan in 1971 and consequently began to build bases in southern Lebanon, eventually forming a so-called Palestinian "state within a state." Israeli security was of course directly threatened. Several incidents between the PLO and Israel during the years 1948–1982 gave the Israelis the justification needed to invade southern Lebanon. The invasion turned into a Lebanese war that lasted until 2000 and had devastating outcomes for all parties involved.[5]

The Palestinian refugee issue in Lebanon has almost entirely been ignored by the EU. Approximately 455,000 refugees, about ten percent of Lebanon's population, reside in Lebanon,[6] and have become a severe human rights problem. The harsh conditions endured by Palestinian refugees must be understood in light of the country's sectarian nature and the fear that their presence would become permanent. Nevertheless, the main human rights obstacle in respect of the refugees is that Lebanon has refused to apply the 1965 League of Arab States Protocol. The Protocol states that Palestinian refugees should enjoy the same rights as the citizens of the host countries. Palestinian refugees in Lebanon are treated as foreigners, meaning that they are restricted from most professions, from owning property, gaining citizenship and from complete freedom of movement.[7] As the constraints on Palestinian refugees in Lebanon could lead to severe domestic turmoil, refugee rights should be of main concern to the EU both in relation to human rights per se but also in regards to neighborhood security.

In relation to security and Lebanon, fighting terrorism is high up on the EU agenda. In Lebanon power is shared between various religious sects and factions that need to be taken into consideration. Boycotting one entire political party in the name of terrorism would mean ignoring the Shi'ite representation of the power system. Even so, it is clear that the EU strives to weaken and disarm Hezbollah (such as in the case of Hamas) even while refusing (unlike the United States) to list Hezbollah as a terrorist organization.[8] The EU's goal to combat terrorism has had little impact and has rather contributed to the political stalemate in Lebanon, where the EU has low-level contact with Hezbollah. There are other factors related to Hezbollah which have complicated EU-Lebanon relations. For example, the support of Hezbollah by Iran and Syria is a complex factor in EU relations. EU-Lebanon relations were further not helped by the intense war between Hezbollah and Israel in 2006 nor by the tense situation between Lebanon and Israel in general. But first and foremost, the EU's low-level contact with Hezbollah and its explicit effort to fight terrorism shows that the EU is more focused on its own security concerns than on actually implementing its normative agenda.[9]

Another internal circumstance which had severe implications for Lebanese society, and which partly led to the withdrawal of Syria, was the aftermath of the assassination of Prime Minister Rafik Hariri in 2005. The assassination triggered a popular resistance movement against the Syrian occupation of the country. Public pressure in the *Cedar Revolution* eventually led to the resignation of the pro-Syrian Prime Minister Omar Karami. The revolution should be understood as a spill-over effect of democratization efforts in other countries during that time, such as Iraq, Georgia and Ukraine. The goals of the opposition were spelled out as:

> a clear timetable for a complete withdrawal of Syrian armed troops and intelligence services (. . .) the removal of Lebanese intelligence chiefs, the appointment of a "neutral" government with the task of preparing parliamentary elections for May 2005, and an international investigation into Hariri's death.[10]

In relation to the on-going demonstrations of the Arab Spring, which will be discussed below, the *Cedar Revolution* should be understood as the most important democratic movement in Lebanese history to date.

In 2007 the EU and Lebanon adopted an Action Plan within the frame of the ENP in order to address the strategic objectives of EU-Lebanese cooperation. The goal was to support Lebanon's reform process in the fields of democracy, human rights, the rule of law and institution-building. The Action Plan is the latest agreement between the parties, following the Country Report of 2005, the National Indicative Program for 2001–2010 and a Country Strategy Paper for 2007–2013 and serves as the most important instrument for EU democracy promotion in Lebanon in recent times. One of the main problems with the Action Plan is that it is only based on country reports, that is, lessons learned, and lacks the ability to effect change. There are also no directives as to how to deal with obvious political issues, such as the under-representation of religious minorities in the government and regional issues like relations between Hezbollah, Syria and Iran.[11]

Despite that, a specific political initiative was undertaken by the Commission in 2007 in order to create a common vision of economic and social development for Lebanese political parties. The EU reports that "The participants managed to reach a consensus on a shared vision for economic and social policies that place equal emphasis on economic growth, equity, regional development and territorial convergence."[12] This initiative was, at its time, seen as rather successful, not least due to the number of political parties that participated, but in the long run had only a minor impact and was not followed up.

EU and Syria

Relations between Syria and the EU have been permeated by the President's and the Baathist regime's repression of its people. Despite temporary gestures of liberalization, the society remains closed and makes the work of international organizations very problematic. This is not to say that the EU procedures were not flawed themselves. The Association Agreement, which was established to promote political change and reform relating to democracy and human rights, was initially stymied in the Syrian case when Germany, the Netherlands and Great Britain disputed the language used in the clause on Weapons of Mass Destruction (WMD). The Association Agreement was seen as a breakthrough in many aspects, but it took place during a very sensitive time when France and the United States were pressuring Syria to withdraw from Lebanon and the UK was expressing concern over Syria's support for Iraqi rebels, and immediately hit a dead-lock. Moreover the EU's requirement for Syrian cooperation in the investigation of the murder of Hariri halted the procedure.[13] The Agreement has still not been signed and ratified. Nevertheless, the EU uses this Agreement to urge both Syria and Lebanon to implement reforms in the areas of democracy and human rights but to little domestic effect (particularly in Syria, where it has not been fully implemented[14]).

Just as in the case of Lebanon, EU policies have been impacted by the historical role of France which affects the local outcome in Syria. During the time of the French mandate vigorous Syrian opposition to an external ruler led to full scale war in 1925. Syria became independent from France in 1946. Ties have remained strong, but at times relations are strained due to Syrian policy in Lebanon, especially pre-2005. Further, French-Syrian relations were particularly frosty during the period around 2007 when France refused to cooperate with Syria until it was clear that Syria was not involved in the political crisis in Lebanon. Previously, France had been one of few European countries where demonstrations supporting the leadership of Bashar al-Asad had taken place.[15] But on 7 June 2011 the French foreign minister declared that al-Asad had lost all credibility and was not fit to rule the country.[16]

Syria's internal affairs have in the past been closely linked with events in Lebanon, and vice-versa. Even if Syria seemed to be riding the wave of reform in Lebanon in the aftermath of the 2005 withdrawal, Syrian security forces continued to routinely arrest citizens without charge, torture them during interrogation and imprison them without trial for political reasons. The violations of human rights in Syria cry out for EU involvement, but the lack of transparency, monitors and access to local sources hinder the EU from working successfully. Syrian authorities have systematically prohibited international agencies from conducting any investigations in the country, making futile the role of the international community.[17]

Hope emerged as Bashar al-Asad took over rule after his father Hafiz al-Asad's death in 2000. Human rights organizations appeared on the scene, civil society mobilized and people strove towards change with the EU's rhetorical support. But when the regime feared civil war, development halted and Syria's citizens still enjoy few rights. Since 2003, very few human rights organizations have operated in Syria, thus offering few if any partners for the EU to work with. Even a low figure is misleading since "all of the Human Rights Associations of Syria's research, reports, correspondence and press releases in 2004 were the products of one woman."[18] Syria's lack of capable civil society partners is a core reason as to why European support to civil society in Syria is much more limited than, for example, to Lebanon.

The main aim of EU-Syria cooperation is explained as supporting Syria's domestic reform process since it was launched in 2006 after the withdrawal from Lebanon. The cooperation is first and foremost financial which makes the EU Syria's main trading partner. But a secondary goal also concerns supporting civil society organizations, the rights of children and women and modernizing the judiciary. Other than that, EU-Syria relations are also of regional concern as the EU recognizes Syria to be a key actor in the region on several critical issues. According to the EU, increased regional cooperation with Syria since 2008 led to the establishment of diplomatic relations with Lebanon, indirect peace talks with Israel and closer associations with other Arab neighbors.[19]

An EU initiative for change in Syria was taken through the ENP Instrument, valid 2011–2013. With regard to democracy and human rights, the initiative concerns improving the role of Syrian civil society organizations, increasing social and socio-economic development (decreasing poverty and generating empowerment) and reforming education.[20] But support for economic reform is still a main priority and since the AA is in a deadlock, the implementation of the instrument remains technical and far from a reality.[21]

The main EU cooperation with both Syria and Lebanon is still financial. Even if the EU claims that financial cooperation will eventually lead to improvements in human rights and democratization, it seems as if the EU is using its financial support in order to encourage the two countries (especially Syria) to comply with EU demands. The relatively new dimension concerning human rights and democracy was applied by the Euro-Mediterranean Partnership. However, on the ground the human rights initiative mainly concerned strengthening the rule of law and funding local NGOs through money earmarked for promoting civil society.[22] Cooperation regarding democracy and human rights was developed further in the 1990s when the EU reported progress on women's and children's rights. However, it seems that the EU has not succeeded in influencing the domestic political situation in Syria.[23]

The Arab Spring—EU's Role in Lebanon and Syria

The first anti-regime protests, which began in Tunisia, reached Syria in March 2011 with the public protesting the dictatorship of president al-Assad and the undemocratic policies of the Ba'ath regime. The Syrian government and its security forces have ever since answered with violence towards the demonstrators and more than 3000 civilians have been reported killed.[24] On several occasions, and largely rhetorically, the EU, and particularly EU's High Representative Catherine Ashton, expressed concern for the regime's widespread violations of human rights and violence towards civilians, urging a transition towards democracy.[25] The EU has claimed to condemn, in the strongest terms, what al-Assad and his regime are doing: "the brutal repression must be stopped, detained protesters released, free access by international humanitarian and human rights organizations and media allowed, and a genuine and inclusive national dialogue launched."[26]

The EU was one of the first international actors to take measures against the Syrian regime, but it could have done much more much sooner. For the first four months the measures were more or less entirely rhetorical. Sanctions were only considered at the end of August 2011 when France, Britain, Germany and Portugal proposed a resolution for UN-sanctions, including a weapons' embargo. Sanctions are a powerful and underused weapon in the EU armory. The EU can suspend trade concessions and cut aid programs to any third country that violates human rights. Despite that, the EU was surprisingly silent in the early months of 2011. The EU did adopt a specific declaration in May 2011, namely setting out certain prohibitions for specific people relating to the extreme violence of the Syrian regime, as well as listing people in the regime that were subject to restrictive measures on account of their violence towards civilians.[27] A follow-up statement of additional people came in August 2011.[28] Even so, the EU was more or less an observer to the escalating violence.

What was it then that made the EU move from at best a rhetorical stance to actively imposing sanctions? Perhaps threatening statements by the Syrian regime, particularly the Foreign Minister Walid Muallem, made European governments hesitate. But as Syria is not the first case where the EU has waited rather than acted, it is more likely to be a matter of internal procedures. With over 5,000 Syrians killed and thousands injured and imprisoned since May 2011, EU rhetoric has finally turned into action. The question is why. One explanation could be that they have learned from previous mistakes, but that does not explain why they did not act from the very beginning. Another explanation could be that the EU planned to take restrictive measures much earlier, but that internal unwieldiness held things up. More probably the international community as a whole was hoping for the situation to "resolve itself" and thus spare it from having to meddle in a politically sensitive state affair. The fact that the United States was already involved in Iraq and Afghanistan, and the EU was (over)committed in Libya made it too costly to intervene in Syria as well.

Sanctions should be understood in light of the many EU companies (more than in the United States) which do business with Syria, especially around oil. This would explain why the Unites States imposed a wider range of sanctions on Syria. However, the most credible explanation for the sudden full-fledged intervention is the EU's desire for international credibility given the enormous pressure put on the member states to do something instead of sitting on the sidelines.

The latest report from the EU states that the Security Council was not able to adopt a European backed resolution for Syria as planned as Russia and China vetoed all legally binding measures.[29] European concern over Syria is growing as the possibilities for UN-backed action is decreasing. Simultaneously, the EU has decided to suspend preparations for EU events in Syria and to suspend ongoing bilateral programs (under the ENPI and MEDA).[30] On 18 August 2011 the EU promised further action within the human rights field, including further sanctions against the regime.[31] In September EU foreign ministers imposed an embargo on buying or transporting Syrian crude oil and petroleum and on importing European exchange. Agreements already in force had until November 15 to be completed. Such sanctions will have a serious impact on Syria as the EU is Syria's largest oil export market.[32]

Surprisingly, Syria's neighbor Lebanon remained relatively calm during the political turmoil. This does not mean that Lebanon has been silent since December 2010, but that the protests that took place were on a smaller scale. This is directly related to the national system of power sharing based on religious affiliation, that is, there is not *one* obvious ruler to oppose. Also, it is important to acknowledge that Lebanon has already been through its transition phase of democratic consolidation.[33] Given Lebanon's turbulent past which includes civil war, Syrian and Israeli occupation, the Palestinian refugee issue, etc., it is very likely that Lebanese civil society considers a new revolution to be more trouble than it is worth. Moreover Lebanon is sensitive to a number of issues where internal instability can have spill-over effect. These issues include relations with Israel, Syria and Hezbollah, Christian versus Muslim, etc.

Other places where the Arab Spring has passed more or less unnoticed, for similar reasons as in Lebanon, are Jordan, Algeria and Morocco. All three countries have suffered from a violent past where they have reached some sort of democratic status quo, such as Jordan's embryonic parliamentarian elections. However, these countries do not have Lebanon's consociationalist-confessional system. Jordan and Morocco are both governed by one man. This would explain why the Arab Spring was slightly more visible (and led to constitutional reforms) in Jordan and Morocco, than in Lebanon or Algeria. Iraq should be understood as a related phenomenon where a similar potential outcome could occur if the protests are allowed to escalate freely.

The protesters in Lebanon did not encounter the same violent response from the government as those in other countries. By not attracting the same worldwide attention, Lebanon made it possible for the world, including the EU, to rather focus on its neighbor Syria. However, Lebanese political obstacles relating to Syria are rankling. Assad's iron grip on Syria has divided the close ties between Hamas and Hezbollah. Hamas does not support the current violence by the Syrian regime towards its civilians while Hezbollah fears that if the regime falls, the strongest governmental resistance to Israel would be lost. Hezbollah also fears internal Syrian struggle between factions which are non-beneficial to Hezbollah.[34]

As a general response to the Arab revolts the EU Commission launched "A New Response to a Changing Neighborhood" on 25 May 2011. The document underlines "mutual accountability and a shared commitment to the universal values of human rights, democracy and the rule of law."[35] Such a statement is in itself not extraordinary, but it states that "each partner country (to) develop its links with the EU as far as its own aspirations, needs and capacities allow."[36] Hence, if Syria and/or Lebanon ask for assistance the EU will provide greater support for a number of issues, such as democracy and civil and human rights. While the initiative rests with each country, support will be tailored according to the goals and needs of each. The document also states that if governments violate human rights and democracy standards, the EU will apply targeted sanctions and other policy measures (not specified) and in parallel increase its support for civil society institutions. The document should be understood as denoting a fundamental change in the EU's external approach but not to specific policies relating to each country.[37]

Implications and Recommendations for the EU

EU rhetoric in promoting democracy and human rights in Lebanon and Syria does not correspond to its actions. The obstacles seem to be a combination of the EU's own procedures and agendas and specific obstacles within the targeted regimes. It is striking that the EU has been specific and technical on economic and financial cooperation, but vague on democracy and human rights.

As for obstacles within the targeted regimes, Lebanon, for example, is difficult to manage due its turbulent past and dualist structure. The fact that minorities get their voices heard could be considered positive, but internally it is widely criticized since the influence of minorities is after all minimal. Also, the Shi'ites (Hezbollah) make structural change impossible. As Javier Solana has pointed out, trying do demilitarize Hezbollah could be a step towards a viable democratic state. But to simply exclude an important existing political party in negotiations would have counter-effects in the end. Hezbollah does not have to win, since it has already done that. It only has to survive as a potent force.

Even if Lebanon does not have the same authoritarian set-up as Syria or other countries in the region, the EU has still not managed to influence the political situation. Lebanon can be understood as a missed opportunity for the EU which could have ridden the wave of the Arab Spring but instead chose to keep a low profile.

The main worry regarding Syria is that the violence will transform into a prolonged civil war with no winner. With Syrian regime continuing to violently suppress any forms of dissent, the Arab League sought to mediate the conflict at the end of 2011 in order to prevent further violence and imposed a set of sanctions on the Syrian regime in an effort to force it to undertake reforms and meet the demands of the protestors. In December 2011, Arab League dispatched a mission to Syria to monitor events but so far it has failed to gain the confidence of either the protesters or the Syrian military. Instead, the violence has continued unabated. Assuming an intensified conflict, it is likely that the EU will intervene with tough measures, such as in the case of Libya. A second scenario could be the fall of the regime. In such a case it is very important that the transitional government be guided by the international community in fields such as human rights, etc., to enable it to uphold its obligations. In the likelihood of regime fall, the EU should play an important role in preventing acts of revenge and escalating violence. There are attempts by the Syrian opposition movement to create an Interim Transitional National Council (TNC) which would be helpful in establishing a path towards security and progress in a post-Assad period. It would be important for the international community, such as the EU, to show its full support for such a Council, both for the sake of the Syrian population but also for its own sake. Even if Syria is a core player for peace and stability in the region, it is naïve to think that it will suddenly be a good neighbor when so far it has failed to respect the rights of its own citizens.

Notes

1. Reinoud Leenders and Eva Goes, "Promoting Democracy and Human Rights in Lebanon and Syria," in *Crescent of Crisis: U.S.-European Strategy for the Greater Middle East*, ed. Ivo Daalder, Nicole Gnesotto, and Philip Gordon (Washington, D.C: The Brookings Institution, 2006), 94.

2. Traboulsi Fawwaz, *A Modern History of Lebanon* (London: Pluto Press, 2007) 76, 88–89.

3. Ibid., 38, 46.

4. Middle East Watch, *Syria Unmasked: The Suppression of Human Rights by the Asad Regime* (New Haven & London: Yale University Press, 1991), 3–4 and 8–12.

5. Gregory S. Mahler, and Alden R. W. Mahler, *The Arab Israeli Conflict: An Introduction and Documentary Reader* (Oxon: Routledge, 2010), 22–23.

6. UNRWA Official Webpage, "Lebanon," accessed October 10, 2011, http://www.unrwa.org/etemplate.php?id=65

7. Helena Lindholm-Schulz, *The Palestinian Diaspora: Formation of Identities and Politics of Homeland* (London: Routledge, 2003), 53–62.

8. Leenders and Goes, "Promoting Democracy," 94–108.

9. Nathalie Tocci, "The Impact of Western Policies towards Hamas and Hezbollah: What Went Wrong?" in *Political Islam and European Foreign Policy: Perspectives from Muslim Democrats of the Mediterranean*, ed. Michael Emerson and Richard Youngs (Brussels: Centre for European Policy Studies, 2007), 136–59.

10. Karim Knio, "Lebanon: Cedar Revolution or Neo-Sectarian Partition?" *Mediterranean Politics* 10, no. 2 (2005): 225–31.

11. Peter Seeberg, "EU og Naboerne—Mellemosten. Israel, Jordan, Libanon, Palestinensiske Selvstyreområder, Syrien" (Odense: Center for Mellomöststudier, 2009).

12. Delegation of the European Union to the Republic of Lebanon, "Case Studies," accessed August 17, 2011, http://eeas.europa.eu/delegations/lebanon/projects/case_studies/index_en.htm.

13. Anja Zorob, "Partnership with the European Union: Hopes, Risks and Challenges for the Syrian Economy" in *Demystifying Syria*, ed. Fred H. Lawson (London: SOAS, 2009), 144–57.

14. Leenders and Goes, "Promoting Democracy," 94–108.

15. Bassel F. Salloukh, "Demystifying Syrian Policy under Bashar al-Asad," in *Demystifying Syria*, ed. Fred H. Lawson (London: SOAS, 2009), 159–72.

16. "French Declare that Bashar al-Assad has Lost all Legitimacy," *The Telegraph*, accessed September 6, 2011, http://www.telegraph .co.uk/news/worldnews/middleeast/syria/8561445/French-declare-that-Bashar-al-Assad-has-lost-all-legitimacy.html.

17. Middle East Watch, *Syria Unmasked*, 135–45.

18. Joshua Landis and Joe Pace, "The Syrian Opposition: The Struggle from Unity and Relevance, 2003–2008," in *Demystifying Syria*, ed. Fred H. Lawson (London: SOAS, 2009), 122.

19. European Union, "European Neighborhood and Partnership Instrument: Syrian Arab Republic, National Indicative Programme 2011–2013," accessed September 5, 2011, http://ec.europa.eu/world/enp/pdf/country/2011_enpi_nip_syria_en.pdf

20. European Union, "European Neighborhood."

21. European Union, "European Neighborhood."

22. Steven N. Simon, "Declawing the Party of God," *World Policy Journal* 18, no. 2 (2001): 31–42.

23. Leenders and Goes, "Promoting Democracy," 94–108.

24. "UN Rights Chief: Death Toll in Syria Protest Crackdown Exceeds 3,000," *Haaretz*, 14 October, 2011 accessed October 14, 2011, http://www.haaretz.com/news/middle-east/un-rights-chief-death-toll-in-syria-protest-crackdown-exceeds-3-000-1.389945

25. European Union, "Statement by the High Representative Catherine Ashton on Syria," accessed August 19, 2011, http://consilium .europa.eu/uedocs/cms_data/docs/pressdata/EN/foraff/124170.pdf

26. European Union, "Statement by the High Representative Catherine Ashton on Syria," accessed August 19, 2011, http://consilium .europa.eu/uedocs/cms_data/docs/pressdata/EN/foraff/124170.pdf

27. Official Journal of the European Union, "Council Decision 2011/273/CFSP," accessed August 17, 2011, http://eurlex.europa.eu/LexUriServ/LexUriServ.do?uri=OJ:L:2011:121:0011:0014:EN:PDF.

28. Official Journal of the European Union, "Council Decision 2011/488/CFSP," accessed September 2, 2011, http://eurlex.europa .eu/LexUriServ/LexUriServ.do?uri=OJ:L:2011:199:0074:0075:EN:PDF.

29. "Russia and China Veto UN Resolution against Syrian Regime," *The Guardian*, 15 October, 2011, accessed October 15, 2011, http://www.guardian.co.uk/world/2011/oct/05/russia-china-veto-syria-resolution.

30. Delegation of the European Union to Syria, "Upcoming EU Events," accessed October 12, 2011, http://eeas.europa.eu/delegations/syria/press_corner/upcoming_eu_events/index_en.htm.

31. European Union, "Statement by the High Representative Catherine Ashton on Behalf of the EU on EU Action Following the Escalation of Violent Repression in Syria," accessed August 17, 2011, http://www.consilium.europa.eu/uedocs/cms_Data/docs/pressdata/en/cfsp/124393.pdf.

32. "EU Bans Syrian Oil as Protests Continue," *New York Times*, 15 September 2011, accessed September 15, 2011, http://www.nytimes.com/2011/09/03/world/middleeast/03syria.html.

33. Larry Diamond, "Causes and Effects," in *Political Culture and Democracy in Developing Countries*, ed. Larry Diamond (Boulder and London: Lynne Rienner Publishers, 1993), 411–35.

34 ."Will Hezbollah Desert Assad Before the End?" *The Guardian*, 16 September, 2011, accessed September 16, 2011, http://www.guardian.co.uk/commentisfree/2011/aug/28/will-hezbollah-desert-assad.

35. European Commission, "A New Response to a Changing Neighborhood. A Review of European Neighborhood Policy," accessed August 29, 2011, http://ec.europa.eu/world/enp/pdf/com_11_303_en.pdf.

36. European Commission, "A New Response to a Changing Neighborhood. A Review of European Neighborhood Policy," accessed August 29, 2011, http://ec.europa.eu/world/enp/pdf/com_11_303_en.pdf.

37. European Commission, "A New Response to a Changing Neighborhood. A Review of European Neighborhood Policy," accessed August 29, 2011, http://ec.europa.eu/world/enp/pdf/com_11_303_en.pdf.

8

Gulf Cooperation Council (GCC) Countries and Yemen

Tobias Schumacher

During the first half of 2011, Bahrain and Yemen witnessed unprecedented demonstrations, sit-ins, violent clashes between demonstrators and police and security forces, and an attack on the Yemeni presidential compound, which resulted in the death of the Yemeni Speaker of the Parliament, Abdullah Bin Hussein al-Ahmar, and in serious injuries to Yemeni President Saleh. However, none of these developments, not even the temporary hospitalization of President Saleh in Saudi Arabia, set in motion a process of political liberalization or even led to the fall of the ruling regimes. While the governments of the neighboring Gulf Cooperation Council (GCC) countries expressed their concern that the situation in Yemen might escalate, the Qatari regime and its counterpart in the UAE supported, at least rhetorically, the outbreak of what is widely referred to as an Arab Spring.[1] At the same time, the joint engagement of UAE and Saudi military forces in Bahrain, helping the Al Khalifa regime to clamp down on domestic pro-democracy groups, demonstrated clearly the limits of GCC regimes' support, as well as their determination to resort to violent means once the authoritarian foundations of the Gulf monarchies were endangered.

Conversely, the GCC countries' relations with their external, non-regional partners were, by and large, not affected by these developments. Like the United States, which exploited the power vacuum in Yemen to undertake air strikes against terrorist suspects,[2] the European Union's initial reaction to the developments in Bahrain and Yemen was marked by surprise and then hesitation. As was already the case when the uprisings in Tunisia and Egypt broke out, the European Union (EU) adopted a wait-and-see approach before it finally resorted to an extremely narrow policy mix based on declaratory statements and a few regional missions by the High Representative of the EU for Foreign Affairs and Security Policy/Vice-President of the European Commission (HRVP) and some governmental representatives of EU member states.

Against this background, this chapter looks at the role the EU has played in promoting human rights, democracy, good governance, and the rule of law in the Gulf region, here understood as the region encompassing the six member states of the GCC and Yemen, up until early 2011. It argues that both before and during the latest uprisings in the MENA region, EU policies towards the GCC countries and Yemen as regards democracy and human rights promotion, broadly speaking, have been highly ineffective. This is mainly due to differences in the bargaining powers of the EU and the GCC, the endurance of the strained relationship between individual and common interests in the EU's foreign policy, and due to a considerable strategic neglect of the Gulf region as a whole on the part of the EU and many of its member states.

The chapter argues that the participation of the EU, the GCC countries, and Yemen in intergovernmental cooperation frameworks, such as the EU-GCC partnership and the EU-Yemen cooperation framework, has not impacted favorably on human rights and democracy standards in these countries. The underlying assumption behind the arguments presented below is that a gap exists between the EU's official self-imposed objective to pursue and, in fact, deepen, a normative foreign policy agenda towards the Gulf countries on the one hand, and on the other a policy practice, strongly influenced by the "logic of diversity,"[3] characterized by diverging foreign policy interests of the EU member states' governments, that puts commercial and stability-related aspects at its core.

Human Rights and Democracy Promotion in EU-GCC Relations from 1989 to 2011

When the then European Economic Community (EEC) and its member states and the six GCC countries signed the EEC-GCC cooperation agreement in 1988, issues relating to political reform were not anticipated as playing a role in their future relations. Cooperation agreements offered to non-EEC member states as part of the EEC's development cooperation policies of the 1970s and 1980s usually contained no reference to political matters and potentially sensitive areas beyond commercial, economic, and technical matters were excluded. Hence, the agreement with the GCC focuses exclusively on these three sectors and is furthermore intended to "strengthen the process of economic development and diversification of the GCC countries and [to] reinforce the role of the GCC in contributing to peace and stability in the region."[4] The only reference that hints at the possibility of a potentially larger scope can be found in article 1(a) which envisages the general strengthening of "relations between the European Economic Community, on the one hand, and the GCC countries, on the other, by placing them in an institutional and contractual framework."[5] While this stipulation is sufficiently broad to accommodate at least some form of political interaction on human rights and democracy issues, it took until 1995 for the EU and the GCC to—albeit reluctantly—refer to article 1(a) for the first time.

On 20 July 1995, the first ever EU-GCC Ministerial Troika meeting took place in Granada with a view to identifying ways and means to overcome the lack of progress in the free trade negotiations between the two sides and to reinvigorate inter-regional relations. Beyond the identified need to expand economic cooperation and to develop instruments of cooperation in the cultural and scientific fields, it was agreed to set up an EU-GCC dialogue, though its frequency and scope were not defined. The European Commission, in search of a more influential and political role both within the new EU structure, as defined by Maastricht, and the seemingly important inter-regional configuration, seized the opportunity and in November 1995, only five days before the Barcelona Summit inaugurating the Euro-Mediterranean Partnership, published an ambitious communication to the Council outlining its position on the future shape of relations. For the first time in EU-GCC relations, the Commission evoked the notion of shared political and security interests, emphasized the need to regard the GCC as a region of strategic importance to the EU, and called upon EU member states to improve qualitatively the entire relationship. According to the Commission, an integral part of such an upgrade should have been the setting up of decentralized cooperation programs at civil society level and, most of all, a "frank and constructive discussion"[6] of human rights and democracy issues.

However, at the 6th Joint EU-GCC Council, which took place just a few months after the communication was published, no real progress was made as regards the implementation of the Commission's lofty ambitions in the human rights and democracy field. Indeed, the Joint Council conclusions of 22 April 1996 contained a paragraph in which both sides stress their commitment to the promotion of human rights. Yet, this was contradicted by a reference, included on the insistence of the GCC countries, that noted "the diversity of systems of values"[7] and hence the enormous differences that exist in what constitutes a common understanding of human rights and their promotion. In fact, almost all the Joint Council conclusions adopted ever since contain either an explicit reference to the "national and regional particularities and their various historical, cultural and religious backgrounds"[8] or a simple stipulation recognizing their cultural diversities.

Until 2001, all relevant human rights and democracy-related references were extremely short and rather superficial. However, in the wake of the events of 9/11 and greater pressure on authoritarian regimes in the MENA to commit themselves to political reforms, the tone and substance of human rights and democracy-related references in EU-GCC Joint Council conclusions changed as a consequence of more determined efforts by the EU and some member states to link the issue to the ongoing free trade negotiations. For example, in the 12th EU-GCC Joint Council conclusions both sides noted "that the events of

11 September made it imperative to ensure an open dialogue on issues, including the protection of human rights, which could contribute to better mutual knowledge."[9] The 13th EU-GCC Joint Council conclusions contained an explicit reference to the then deliberations within the GCC to establish a Human Rights Round Table, adding that such a Round Table "would facilitate dialogue between the GCC and the EU on human rights issues."[10] The joint communiqué issued on 17 May 2004 was even more advanced, as it declared formally for the first time since the cooperation agreement entered into force in 1989 that both sides had agreed "on the importance of close and effective cooperation on human rights." What is more, it stipulated that an agreement was reached "to incorporate in the FTA [Free Trade Agreement] clauses on human rights and migration, and [that the parties] invited negotiators to conclude negotiations on these elements as soon as possible."[11] Also, "they expressed their shared willingness to enter into a dialogue on human rights and invited officials to exchange views on what mechanisms could be used for such a purpose."[12] In conjunction with the fact that the same communiqué for the first time touched upon political participation in GCC countries, it was the most wide-ranging official acknowledgement as regards future cooperation in the field of human rights and governance that both sides had ever adopted. The post-9/11 climate, together with the international community's new democracy promotion agenda, led to a few signs of political liberalization in some countries in the Gulf—mainly in Bahrain and Kuwait—and to a growing intra-Arab discourse on political reform. It also contributed to the GCC countries' willingness to go beyond the superficial rhetoric of the past. Such progress is particularly noteworthy given the decision in 2002 by the European Commission to discontinue decentralized Gulf-related civil society programs, most of which had hardly commenced anyway. In light of the widespread hope that "springtime for Arab democracy"[13] had finally arrived, the following Manama Joint Council and ministerial meeting of April 2005 picked up on the overall dynamic and discussed human rights, NGOs, and their role in overseeing and even implementing relevant UN conventions and national laws.[14]

However, since then, all EU-GCC Joint Council and ministerial meetings have failed to build on previously made commitments. The reasons for this lack of progress are manifold:
First, all regimes in the Gulf are primarily interested in regime
durability and consider a true and meaningful engagement in a
human rights and democracy-related dialogue with the EU and
its member states as potentially counterproductive. Over the
past 16 years, Saudi Arabia has been at the forefront of those
opposing any inter-regional or bilateral cooperation on human
rights and democracy-related issues and regularly tries to shift
the debate to a coordination of positions on international issues,
especially Palestine.[15] Although often exposed to some sort of
bullying by the GCC's largest and most powerful member and
therefore not always in line with Riyadh, smaller GCC member
states find Saudi Arabia's outspoken reluctance rather useful as
it allows them to pursue a more liberal-minded rhetoric abroad,
mainly to please their Western partners, without being forced to
act upon it domestically.

Second, for years, some EU member states linked the issue of
human rights and democracy to the negotiations of an FTA (Free
Trade Agreement) whereas GCC countries regarded the latter
as the first step towards political cooperation and the possible
initiation of a human rights and democracy-related dialogue.
As a result, FTA negotiations are repeatedly suspended by GCC
countries, the latest example of which occurred in May 2010
when GCC countries complained about this issue-linkage and
disagreed with the EU's demands on petrochemical subsidies
and foreign companies holding majority stakes in GCC companies.[16] Also, the insistence on the part of the EU to condition
the FTA has increasingly led GCC states to turn elsewhere and
establish alternative relations with actors (such as China and
India) that are solely interested in commercial cooperation.

Third, EU member states' governments themselves are in
disagreement over the approach the EU should take towards
the GCC. Officially, they all support the EU's line of upholding
and promoting its values and interests and of protecting human
rights, as expressed in article 2 (5) of the Lisbon Treaty. However, in the pursuit of their national foreign policies towards

Gulf countries, they tend to subordinate this commitment to the upholding of their multi-faceted national interests. Apart from the fact that EU member states' governments in the context of the FTA negotiations turned out to be divided into protectionists and free trade proponents, France and the United Kingdom repeatedly undermined EU calls for political reform in the Gulf. By engaging in multi-billion dollar arms deals, the latest of which is exemplified in France's current negotiations with the UAE over the sale of 60 Rafale fighter jets worth approximately 4-5 billion Euro, they rather contribute to the persistence of authoritarian rule in the region and counteract official EU policy.[17]

Fourth, with the exception of Yemen, and the two GCC members Bahrain and Kuwait, no GCC country has ratified either the International Covenant on Civil and Political Rights or the International Covenant on Economic, Social and Cultural Rights. In conjunction with the reluctance of most GCC countries and Yemen to cooperate with United Nations bodies in the field of human rights and democracy promotion, this seriously questions the overall credibility of the envisaged EU-GCC human rights dialogue.

Human Rights and Democracy Promotion in EU-Yemen Relations

As far as cooperation with Yemen in the field of human rights and democracy promotion is concerned, the EU and its member states have for a long time been even more reluctant to engage seriously, not least due to the fact that Yemen—long considered a "heavily indebted country"—was not regarded either by the EU or its member states as strategically relevant. This perception changed only in the wake of the events of 9/11. Since then, there has been greater awareness on the part of both the European Commission and EU member states' governments—as reflected in the opening of a full diplomatic EU representation in Sana'a in late 2009—about the fact that the mix of widespread poverty, social exclusion, absent democratic institutions, intra-tribal and tribal-governmental conflicts, and infrastructural deficiencies, in conjunction with a contested monopoly on the state's use of force, may pose a security risk and also have negative repercussions on other GCC countries and Europe.

Like EU-GCC relations, EU-Yemen relations are based on a cooperation agreement. This was signed in 1984 and replaced in July 1998 by an agreement on commercial, development, and economic cooperation. However, in contrast to the EU-GCC cooperation agreement, it is more inclusive and wide-ranging in so far as it contains more areas of cooperation. It stipulates that both parties refer to the relevant legal instruments in the field of human rights and base their relations "on respect of democratic principles and fundamental human rights."[18] Moreover, article 18 refers explicitly to the non-execution of the agreement and allows both parties to "take appropriate measures"[19] if the other party fails to fulfill any of its obligations under the agreement.

According to EU sources, since the unification of Yemen in May 1990, the EU has committed approximately EUR180 million to the country, the majority to finance projects in the field of food, security, and economic development.[20] After the events of 9/11, the EU grafted parts of the Euro-Mediterranean Partnership's political charter onto its relations with Yemen. Accordingly, the European Commission's country strategy paper 2002–2006 defined good governance, democracy, and human rights as one of the four priority areas of cooperation; the Commission's Strategy Paper 2007–2013 reiterates this importance. During 2007–2010, financial aid provided by the EU to support the development of a sound electoral framework, to strengthen the parliament, political parties, the judiciary, rule of law, and compliance with human rights amounted to EUR19.5 million. Governance and human rights issues are regularly discussed in the framework of the political dialogue that was established in 2003 and in the annual Joint Consultative committees. Nonetheless, the EU's European Instrument for Democracy and Human Rights (EIDHR) still does not identify Yemen as a priority country and the only initiative that it ever financed in Yemen was a training of domestic security forces.[21] Also, in spite of the regular bilateral consultations and like all the financial aid that the EU has provided since the formal establishment of diplomatic relations in 1978, it was never conditional upon compliance with article 1 of the cooperation agreement or with the continuation of the country's liberalization process that began in the early 1990s and was terminated only a few years later.

The main reasons for this approach are threefold. First, Germany, the United Kingdom, France, the Netherlands, Poland, and the Czech Republic enjoy privileged relations and throughout the years have been the key supporters of steady EU engagement—at the expense of a strict interpretation of the relevant human rights stipulation of the cooperation agreement. Second, since 1993 the EU has managed to maintain and increase a considerable trade surplus with Yemen (EUR108 billion in 2009).[22] Any suspension of the cooperation agreement due to Yemen's non-compliance with human rights and governance standards would most likely lead to a suspension of the mutually agreed trade preferences and therefore jeopardize the trade surpluses of the EU, affecting Germany, France, and the United Kingdom most significantly. Third, the issue of counter-terrorism cooperation has increasingly entered the agenda of EU-Yemen relations in the last decade. On account of this development, the EU and some of its member states, most of all the United Kingdom and France, currently focus on closer security and anti-terrorism cooperation rather than on human rights and democracy promotion, trusting that this will prevent Yemen from turning into a safe haven for terrorist cells.[23]

EU Human Rights and Democracy
Promotion Policies during the Arab Spring

Bahrain

The EU's response to the protests and violence that erupted in Manama in mid-February 2011 is characterized by an almost exclusive recourse to declaratory statements/conclusions, issued either by Catherine Ashton and the EU Foreign Affairs Council or the foreign ministries of some member states. Following a standard procedure, the first EU statements were marked by caution and some degree of restraint. This allowed the EU to win some time, undertake a situation analysis as events unfolded, and determine whether it was necessary to toughen its rhetoric. However, neither in February or March, when the clashes between protesters and Bahraini security forces were most violent, nor in the wake of a decision taken on 28 April by a Bahraini military court to sentence four Shi'a Bahraini nationals to death for the alleged murder of two police officers, did the EU opt for a tougher wording. Instead, until the end of July it repeated itself by "[deploring] the use of violence by the Bahraini security forces and [...] the loss of lives,"[24] by calling "on all parties to exercise restraint and calm,"[25] by urging the "government and the security forces [to] respect and protect the human rights of peaceful protestors, including freedom of expression and freedom of assembly," and by urging "all parties to engage rapidly in meaningful dialogue with a view to bringing about reforms which offer real prospects for successfully addressing the country's challenges."[26] The last statement in particular is noteworthy, as it captures the EU's position: as in the case of Yemen, the EU stressed the need for reforms and demanded that the Bahraini regime engage in comprehensive and inclusive dialogue. Yet, it stopped short of defining more precisely the character of reforms and the challenges it refers to and of calling for a transition and thus the resignation of King Hamad bin Isa Al Khalifa and his ruling family.

Any political transition process in Bahrain may mean that the country's Shi'ite majority obtains more power. However, as the EU and numerous member states' governments, most notably those of Britain, France, and Germany, fear that such a development would help those Iranian factions that conceive of Bahrain as Iran's fourteenth province achieve greater influence over domestic Bahraini and eventually regional politics,[27] no agreement could be reached within the EU Foreign Affairs Council to adopt more far-ranging language or to dispatch a fact-finding mission. This disagreement can also be explained by the fact that, as in the case of Yemen, the house of Al Khalifa had throughout the years proven to be a reliable partner for European arms producers. Although both the United Kingdom and France temporarily suspended their arms sales to Bahrain in early 2011, both countries have been engaged in arms cooperation and defense assistance and do not wish to see this engagement disrupted. For example, in 2009 and 2010, the United Kingdom and France, together with Belgium, Sweden, and Germany, sold the Al Khalifa regime weapons amounting to more than EUR45 million.[28]

This background explains why the EU refrained from condemning the Bahraini regime at the 21st Joint EU-GCC Council and Ministerial meeting, held in Abu Dhabi on 20 April 2011, and why both blocs have ignored yet again calls by international human rights organizations, such as the Bahrain Center for Human Rights or the International Federation for Human Rights (FIDH), to insert a human rights clause into both existing and future agreements and making it an essential precondition to relations.[29] In this context, it is also almost natural that the engagement of Saudi and UAE military forces in Bahrain was not discussed either and that King Al Khalifa in a personal meeting with Catherine Ashton on the sidelines of the EU-GCC Joint Council and Ministerial meeting rejected any discussion that touched upon the root causes of unrest, that is, authoritarianism, in both Arab Mediterranean countries and the Gulf.

Yemen

In response to the outbreak of demonstrations by large segments of Yemeni society in early 2011 against the dictatorial rule of President Saleh and subsequent clashes between forces loyal to the regime, rival elites, and protesters, the EU through Catherine Ashton, the EU's Foreign Affairs Council, and various member states' governments, has been resorting exclusively to declaratory statements. The first such statement was made on 17 February by Ashton's spokesperson and clearly reflects the uncertainty that characterized the general mood in both the European Commission and the Council with respect to the potential impact these clashes may have on the stability of Yemen and its fragile security situation. While the use of violence and the loss of life were strongly deplored, Ashton initially used rather cautious language, demanding only that all parties engage in a "genuine, comprehensive and inclusive national dialogue."[30] No reference was made to Yemen's human rights obligations and the need to undertake wide-ranging political reforms, leading to a fully fledged democratization, was only hinted at. However, only three days later another declaration was issued. It singled out the Yemeni authorities and by extension the security and armed pro-government forces as responsible for the violence. Moreover, in the declaration, the EU recalled "Yemen's obligations to protect the rights to life and security of the person, and the rights to freedom of expression, association, and peaceful assembly" and demanded "the implementation of genuine political reforms."[31] On 12 March, Ashton stressed for the first time that the Yemeni government is "accountable for the welfare and safety of its people"[32]; on 21 March, the EU's Foreign Affairs Council went even further by pointing to the need for "orderly transition" and by threatening to review EU and member states' policies "should the safety of demonstrators not be ensured."[33]

To date, six months into the first Foreign Affairs Council conclusions on the unrest in Yemen, a total of 11 statements by Catherine Ashton and three conclusions by the EU's Foreign Affairs Council have been adopted. Apart from the fact that the EU is nowadays explicitly supporting the GCC initiative according to which President Saleh should hand over power to Vice-President Abd-Rabbu Mansour Hadi in exchange for impunity,[34] all documents contain the same language and repeat what was stated by the Council and Ashton in March 2011. While they stress the need for political reform, they have not used either their declarations or the EU-Yemen political dialogue mechanism to specify the contents of such reform.

In contrast to its announcement to review EU policies towards Yemen and to hold the Yemeni regime fully responsible for the escalation of violence, the EU Foreign Affairs Council has not increased its pressure on the regime. Instead of suspending the cooperation agreement or even imposing sanctions, it still considers the elite close to President Saleh as the EU's main interlocutor. This practice underscores the intra-EU fragmentation over how to address in practical terms the country's much demanded political transition and is proof of the fact that since the entering-into-force of the 1998 cooperation agreement, the EU has been unable to strengthen and support civil society actors and opposition movements that could act as alternative actors of change. That the EU and its member states continue to support members of Saleh's regime and still shy away from imposing sanctions must be attributed to the security narrative that dominates the discourse in Brussels and some EU capitals. The most prominent example of such thinking was offered by British Foreign Minister William Hague, who in early June remarked that Yemen "could become a much more serious threat to our own national security"[35] if Al-Qaeda in the Arabian Peninsula (AQAP) exploited the situation. Such notions explain why numerous EU member states, most recently Bulgaria, the United Kingdom, the Czech Republic, and France, have for years been ignoring the EU Code of Conduct on Arms Exports of 1998, thereby tacitly accepting, and contributing to, the ongoing suppression of Yemeni opposition movements.[36]

Conclusion

The EU's efforts to promote democracy, human rights, good governance, and the rule of law in the six GCC countries and Yemen in the last twenty years have thrown into question the EU's political will to take seriously the EU-GCC Joint Council and Ministerial conclusions. Although the Treaty of Lisbon increased the EU's potential room for maneuver in the international arena, neither the newly established HRVP nor EU member states' governments have made use of these new possibilities. This can be attributed to the increasingly assertive behavior of GCC states and their geostrategic independence from Europe. Since the GCC countries signed the EU-GCC cooperation agreement in 1988, they have successfully diversified their diplomatic relations and nowadays engage in partnerships that do not force them to enter into political and human rights dialogue. Although the EU is the GCC countries' second most important trading partner, the last two decades have proven that Gulf regimes are not prepared to make substantial concessions in the field of human rights and democracy even if such an approach has negative repercussions on their trade relations with EU member states. At the same time, authoritarian rulers in the Gulf have learned throughout these years, in particular during the recent crises in Bahrain and Yemen, that the EU itself is not prepared to increase pressure and use its various channels and instruments to push GCC countries to better comply with human rights and democratic governance standards. Such reluctance on the part of the EU can be attributed to the divergences of interest that exist at the level of the individual EU member states.

To date, no European-level definition exists as to the role the Gulf should play in the EU's foreign policy agenda. A first effort was made in this regard with the adoption of the European Security Strategy in 2003 and the adoption of a Strategic Partnership with the Mediterranean and Middle East in 2004. Since then, however, no further attempts have been made to remedy this shortcoming, with the result that the EU-GCC partnership's official reform component, like the EU action plan framework with Arab Mediterranean countries,[37] is incomplete and conceptually flawed. Good governance and the rule of law are omitted completely from the inter-regional agenda and the language pertaining to democracy and human rights is nebulous and superficial at best. The EU and the GCC countries failed to agree on a commonly accepted definition of these terms and their relationship to one another. What is more, many official EU statements referring to Bahrain, Kuwait, and Yemen stipulate the need for "continued and strengthened democratic reforms"[38] and even praise "the ongoing development of democratic structures,"[39] thus giving the impression that a true democratization process is already underway.

At a time when the EU is immersed in ensuring the survival of the Eurozone and possibly of the Union itself, it may well be forced to turn to capital-rich Gulf monarchies for financial assistance. Naturally, this possibility increases the leverage of these monarchies in relation to the EU, shattering any hopes that societal actors in the Gulf may have had that compliance with human rights and democratic standards might assume a more prominent role in EU-Gulf relations.

Notes

1. As part of this alleged support, both countries participated in the enforcement of UNSC resolution 1973 on Libya calling for an immediate ceasefire and authorizing the international community to establish a no-fly zone and to protect civilians.

2. Mark Mezzetti, "U.S. is intensifying a Secret Campaign of Yemen Airstrikes," *The New York Times,* June 8, 2011.

3. Philip Gordon, "Europe's Uncommon Foreign Policy," *International Security* 22 (1997): 82.

4. Article 1(c), EU-GCC cooperation agreement, published in Official Journal L 054 , February 25, 1989, 3–15. Accessed November 4, 2011, http://trade.ec.europa.eu/doclib/html/140300.htm

5. Article 1(a), ibid.

6. See Communication from the Commission to the Council of November 22, 1995 on improving relations between the European Union and the countries of the Gulf Cooperation Council (GCC), COM(95) 541 final, 5.

7. Conclusions Ministerial Meeting and 6th EU-GCC Joint Council, Luxembourg, April 22, 1996. See Pres. 96/103, April 22, 1996. Accessed November 4, 2011, http://europa.eu/rapid/pressReleasesAction.do? reference=PRES/96/103&format=HTML&aged=1&language=EN&gu iLanguage=en.

8. 17th EU-GCC Joint Council and Ministerial Meeting Joint Communiqué, Riyadh. Accessed November 4, 2011, http://www .europa-eu-un.org/articles/en/article_7013_en.htm

9. 12th EU-GCC Joint Council and Ministerial Meeting Joint Communiqué, Granada. Accessed November 4, 2011, http:// www.consilium.europa.eu/uedocs/cms_data/docs/pressdata/ en/er/69611.pdf

10. 13th EU-GCC Joint Council and Ministerial Meeting Joint Communiqué, Doha. Accessed November 4, 2011, http://www.eeas .europa.eu/gulf_cooperation/docs/13jc.pdf

11. 14th Joint Council and Ministerial Meeting Joint Communiqué, Brussels. Accessed November 4, 2011, http://eeas.europa.eu/gulf _cooperation/docs/14jcf.pdf

12. Ibid.

13. "Springtime for Democracy," *Time Magazine,* March 2, 2005.

14. 15th Joint Council and Ministerial Meeting Joint Communiqué, Manama. Accessed November 4, 2011, http://www.eeas.europa.eu/ gulf_cooperation/docs/finaldecl_050405.pdf

15. Ibrahim Suleiman Al-Duraiby, *Saudi Arabia, GCC and the EU: Limitations and Possibilities for an Unequal Triangular Relationship* (Dubai: GRC Press, 2009).

16. Glen Carey and Wael Mahdi, "GCC States Put EU Free Trade Talks on Hold," *Arabianbusiness.com,* May 26, 2010. Accessed November 4, 2011, http://www.arabianbusiness.com/gcc-states-put-eu-free-trade-talks-on-hold-271018.html.

17. Accessed November 4, 2011, http://www.thepeninsulaqatar.com/q/55-khalid-al-jaber/128219-gcc-arms-race-an-issue-of-safety-and-stability.html On the issue of bilateral relations between some EU member states and GCC countries, see Giacomo Luciani and Tobias Schumacher, *Relations Between the European Union and the Gulf Cooperation Council States. Past Record and Promises for the Future* (Dubai: GRC Press, 2004).

18. Article 1, Cooperation Agreement between the European Union and the Republic of Yemen. See Official Journal of the European Communities L72/18, March 11, 1998.

19. Article 18, ibid.

20. "European Commission Development and Cooperation: Yemen,". Accessed November 4, 2011, http://ec.europa.eu/europeaid/where/gulf-region/country-cooperation/yemen/yemen_en.htm.

21. See EuropeAid "Compendium of Activities funded under EIDHR 2000-2006." Accessed November 4, 2011, http://ec.europa.eu/europeaid/where/worldwide/eidhr/documents/updated_report_by_location_en.pdf

22. Accessed November 4, 2011, http://trade.ec.europa.eu/doclib/docs/2006/september/tradoc_113464.pdf

23. "Council Conclusions on Yemen," last modified November 27, 2009, www.consilium.europa.eu/ueDocs/cms_Data/docs/pressData/en/gena/110779.pdf

24. Statement by EU High Representative Catherine Ashton on the events in Bahrain, February 19, 2011. Accessed November 4, 2011, http://www.eeas.europa.eu/statements/hr/index_en.htm.

25. Ibid.

26. Council conclusions on Bahrain, 3091st Foreign Affairs Council meeting, Brussels, May 23, 2011. Accessed November 4, 2011, http://www.consilium.europa.eu/uedocs/cms_Data/docs/.../122162.pdf.

27. See for example wikileaks, accessed November 4, 2011, http://www.telegraph.co.uk/news/wikileaks-files/8331615/BAHRAIN-AS-IRANS-FOURTEENTH-PROVINCE.html

28. Human Rights Watch, "EU should ban arms sales to Yemen and Bahrain," accessed on November 4, 2011, http://www.hrw.org/news/2011/05/11/eu-should-ban-arms-sales-yemen-and-bahrain

29. See FIDH, Open letter in view of the EU-GCC Joint Cooperation Council, accessed November 4, 2011, http://bahraincenter.blogspot.com/2010_06_01_archive.html

30. Statement by the Spokesperson of EU High Representative Catherine Ashton on Yemen, February 17, 2011. Accessed on November 4, 2011, http://www.eeas.europa.eu/statements/spokes/index_en.htm.

31. Local EU Statement on Yemen, February 20, 2011, accessed November 4, 2011, http://eeas.europa.eu/delegations/yemen/press_corner/all_news/news/2011/20110220_en.htm.

32. Statement by EU High Representative Catherine Ashton on Yemen, Brussels, March 12, 2011. Accessed November 4, 2011, http://www.eeas.europa.eu/statements/hr/index_en.htm.

33. Council conclusions on Yemen, 3076th Foreign Affairs Council meeting, Brussels, March 21, 2011. Accessed November 4, 2011, www.consilium.europa.eu/uedocs/cms_Data/docs/.../120071.pdf

34. The initiative was proposed by the GCC countries' foreign ministers on April 3 to address the political crisis in Yemen. The initiative was signed by the opposition on May 21 and by the ruling party on the following day. President Saleh, however, has repeatedly refused to sign the initiative but said that he would do so if the opposition came to the presidential palace to sign it. On 12 September, Saleh authorized his Vice-President Abd Rabbo Mansour Hadi to sign the initiative on his behalf. Yet, at the time of writing, President Saleh is still in power.

35. William Hague, quoted in www.euobserver.com "EU voices mixed emotions about Yemen revolution," June 6, 2011. Accessed November 4, 2011, http://euobserver.com/24/32442.

36. According to Human Rights Watch, in 2009 alone, Bulgaria sold the Yemeni regime firearms, ammunition, bombs, rockets, and missiles worth EUR 85.9 million. Accessed November 4, 2011, http://www.hrw.org/news/2011/05/11/eu-should-ban-arms-sales-yemen-and-bahrain

37. Raffaella Del Sarto and Tobias Schumacher, "From Brussels with Love: Leverage, Benchmarking, and the Action Plans with Jordan and Tunisia in the EU's Democratization Policy," *Democratization* 18, no. 4 (2011), 932–56.

38. See statement published on the occasion of Catherine Ashton's meeting with the Yemeni Minister of Foreign Affairs, Abu-Bakr Al-Qirbi, on February 2, 2011 in Brussels. Accessed November 4, 2011,

http://europa.eu/rapid/pressReleasesAction.do?reference=MEMO/11/65&format=HTML&aged=0&language=EN&guiLanguage=en

39. See statement on Kuwait by the chair of the European Parliament's relations with the Arab peninsula, Angelika Niebler, on March 2, 2011 in Brussels. Accessed November 4, 2011, http://www.kuna.net.kw/NewsAgenciesPublicSite/ArticleDetails.aspx?id=2142581&Language=en.

9

American Democracy Promotion in the Middle East

Lessons for Europe?

Oz Hassan

In the aftermath of the September 11, 2001 terrorist attacks, the United States increasingly sought to promote democracy in the Middle East and North Africa (MENA). Although this strategy came to be largely associated with the invasion of Iraq, and the belief that a benign domino effect would spread throughout the region, the policy President Obama inherited was far more nuanced. President George W. Bush's legacy was institutional, through the creation of the Middle East Partnership Initiative (MEPI), the Middle East Free Trade Area (MEFTA), and the Broader Middle East and North Africa initiative (BMENA) within the US foreign policy bureaucracy. Furthermore, it was President Bush who codified his democracy promotion strategy in *National Security Presidential Directive 58*, entitled *Institutionalizing the Freedom Agenda*, and who signed the ADVANCE Democracy Act of 2007 into law.[1] By the time President Bush left office, hundreds of millions of dollars had been spent promoting democracy in the MENA, and the United States had declared with the force of law that it would prioritize, along with other foreign policy goals, the promotion of democracy and human rights around the world.[2]

At a superficial level, the so-called "Arab Spring" appears to vindicate President Bush's Freedom Agenda and suggests that

President Obama, and indeed the European Union, should learn lessons from the forty-third president. However, upon closer inspection such an assertion is highly problematic. The 2011 revolutions, rather than vindicating the Freedom Agenda, are in fact the ultimate expression of its failure. The Freedom Agenda was designed to *gradually* reform the region over a period of generations working with "friends" and "partners." The objective was to incrementally transform the region in a stable manner compatible with the pursuit of American interests in the free flow of oil and gas, the movement of military and commercial traffic through the Suez Canal, infrastructure construction projects, the security of regional allies such as Israel and Saudi Arabia, and cooperation on military, counter-terrorism, and counter-proliferation issues.[3] The Arab Spring introduces uncertainty in the pursuit of these interests. It is not clear whether democratic consolidation will take place in Tunisia, Egypt, and Libya, and even if it does, it is not clear that democratization is compatible with America's other interests in the region. The early days of the "spring" brought these issues to the forefront of public consciousness, with Egyptian protesters storming the Israeli embassy in Cairo, Egypt allowing two Iranian warships to transit through the Suez Canal, a Shi'ite uprising in Bahrain generating fears that Iran could gain influence affecting neighboring Saudi Arabia, alarm that Islamists could come to power throughout the region, and increased volatility in the price of oil. Such regional instability and uncertainty is hardly the hallmark of a successful policy. Yet, as the Obama administration attempts to navigate a policy through the changing Middle East mosaic, it is becoming evident that this policy is remarkably similar to previous approaches. This should be of concern to the EU, as this is an area where the EU's goal should be the development of an alternative strategy of engagement with the region.

Democracy Promotion and the Bush Legacy

The formal declaration of the Freedom Agenda by the Bush administration came on November 6, 2003. Addressing the twentieth anniversary of the National Endowment of Democracy (NED), the President announced that:

> Sixty years of Western nations excusing and accommodating the lack of freedom in the Middle East did nothing to make us safe—because in the long run, stability cannot be purchased at the expense of liberty. As long as the Middle East remains a place where freedom does not flourish, it will remain a place of stagnation, resentment, and violence ready for export. And with the spread of weapons that can bring catastrophic harm to our country and to our friends, it would be reckless to accept the status quo.[4]

The "big idea" being espoused was not simply that freedom and democracy should be promoted in the Middle East, but rather that it was in America's national interest to undertake such a task. Tyrannical regimes, it was argued, were providing the conditions for terrorist organizations seeking weapons of mass destruction to recruit and flourish, which posed an existential threat to the US. The administration was arguing that the internal character of states was of concern to American security, and that America's wider regional interests had aligned with American national values.

As the Freedom Agenda became institutionalized, the policy came to embody both *radical* and *conservative* strands. The *radical* dimension of this policy insisted on political democracy, through military regime change if necessary, and was targeted against those that opposed American power and influence in the region. Beyond Iraq, this was expressed in the *Iran Democracy Program* and the *Syria Democracy Program*, which sought to utilize MEPI funds and personnel to bolster internal dissidents and exile groups wanting US-supported regime change. The *conservative* dimension of the policy, however, attempted to broaden the US approach to Middle East reform by focusing on factors outlined in the *2002 UN Arab Human Development Report*. This highlighted a "freedom deficit" in the MENA and argued that a strategy needed to be in place to deliver "freedom from fear" and "freedom from want," in conjunction with educational improvements and women's empowerment in the region. As such, MEPI was constructed to address these issues within its democracy promotion strategy, and was strategically placed within the Department of State's Bureau for Near East Affairs as the central hub for interagency discussions under the Freedom Agenda.

What made this program particularly *conservative*, however, was its emphasis on safeguarding the socio-economic privileges and power of the established autocratic allies in the region. The grand liberal strategy that the Bush administration espoused came with some strong caveats. Senior Bush administration officials were quick to quell notions that a rift with long-term allies such as Saudi Arabia and Egypt had emerged after the launch of the MEPI, arguing that democracy promotion was to be undertaken in "partnership" and designed to offer "positive reinforcement for emerging reform trends."[5] In part, this conservative dimension reflected how MEPI personnel were uncertain how exactly to "promote democracy." As J. Scott Carpenter confessed in his role as overseer of MEPI:

> We don't know yet how best to promote democracy in the Arab Middle East. I mean we just don't know. It's the early days . . . I think there are times when you throw spaghetti against the wall and see if it sticks.[6]

Further, it reflected MEPI's unfamiliarity with regional and internal politics. With most of the personnel being drawn from the "children" of the NED, and having largely dealt with democracy promotion in Russia and Eastern Europe after the fall of the Soviet Union, they relied on longer-term members of the Bureau for Near East Affairs for information. This information was, however, not often forthcoming as there was considerable mid-level opposition from the Department of State, and also the Department of Defense, who highlighted the conflict of interests emerging between democracy promotion and other long-term national interests.[7]

Balancing other interests with the strategic objective of promoting democracy presented the administration with a serious problem. Key figures in the administration consequently turned to the one-size fits all approach of the "Washington Consensus." Promotion of democracy came to mean pushing for elections, opening markets following the prescriptions of neoliberal economics, and pushing for free trade integration within larger interdependent markets in the hope of generating gradual and stable transformation into so-called "market democracies." Within the first few years of the Freedom Agenda's launch, the Bush administration was particularly vocal about pushing for elections. Secretary of State Condoleezza Rice publicly confronted close allies Egypt and Saudi Arabia to hold fair elections, release political prisoners, and allow freedom of expression to women. Moreover, throughout 2004–2006 the Bush administration was keen to represent the Freedom Agenda as a success, arguing that an "Arab spring" was taking place in which there were broad elections in Afghanistan and Iraq; limited elections in Egypt and Saudi Arabia; the "Cedar" revolution in Lebanon which removed Syrian occupational forces; political reforms in Morocco and Jordan; and the introduction of women's suffrage in Kuwait. For the Bush administration such acts were perceived as a vindication of the Freedom Agenda and constituted "extraordinary progress in the expansion of freedom."[8]

However, this situation radically changed in 2006 as the Bush administration lowered the pressure it applied to MENA regimes to hold elections. The Bush administration had failed to foresee the electoral victory of Hamas in the 2006 Palestinian parliamentary elections; this was compounded by Islamic groups hostile to Washington and Israel winning significant gains through elections, including the Muslim Brotherhood in Egypt, Hezbollah in Lebanon, and Shi'ites backed by militias in Iraq. This was coupled with the 2006 Israel-Hezbollah war in Lebanon and increasing civil violence in Iraq despite hopes that the elections would calm the growing insurgency. Under such conditions, the Bush administration reneged on its fragile commitment to pressure autocratic regimes to hold elections, and assumed its well-worn response to a regime in direct opposition to America's hegemony in the region by cutting off aid to the democratically elected Palestinian Authority and refusing to work with the Hamas-led government. Such a response demonstrated that the United States was willing to promote democracy in the Middle East if, and only if, the outcome did not challenge its influence and interests in the region. While Condoleezza Rice had once pronounced the need to move towards democracy, by 2007 domestic reform was barely mentioned. Instead, appreciative comments could be heard about Egypt's support in the region and Saudi Arabia's "moderation."

Consequently, the Freedom Agenda rapidly dropped its emphasis on elections, while retaining a focus on open markets and free trade. Economic initiatives became the central pillar of the agenda. What remained was an incoherent set of policies held together by a neo-liberal core; economic reform was the order of the day, not necessitating serious political reform from partners and allies in the region. This was a key feature of the MEPI funding program under its "economic" reform pillar, as well as of the Bush administration's US-Middle East Free Trade Area (MEFTA). Indeed, announcing MEFTA on May 9, 2003, President Bush argued that:

> The Arab world . . . is largely missing out on the economic progress of our time. . . . So, I propose the establishment of a US-Middle East free trade area within a decade, to bring the Middle East into an expanding circle of opportunity . . . with free markets and fair laws, the people of the Middle East will grow in prosperity and freedom.[9]

For US Trade Representative Robert B Zoellick, MEFTA was perceived to be a key element of America's "competitive liberalization strategy," which would make an assault on protectionism and encourage countries eager for greater access to US markets to fight for Washington's attention and approval.[10] For MENA's autocratic regimes this form of liberalization has typically been part of a regime-driven survival strategy, which in the past allowed governments to avoid legitimation crises by diffusing popular dissatisfaction. By the time President Bush left office, it was clear that the Freedom Agenda was pursuing an "economics-first" strategy in which it envisaged that a gradual modernization process would take place leading to democratic peace. Alternatively, MENA regimes were hoping that a modernization process would allow them to construct Beijing modeled liberal autocracies. Rather than challenging the political power of friendly regimes, the Bush administration was working with them, in "partnership," to carefully and slowly liberalize their autocracies and create the conditions for potential future reform. The Freedom Agenda's conservative strand was relying on gradual economic sequencing to produce democratization. Free trade and free market benefits were seen not only as a method of reducing poverty and unemployment, but as a way of linking economic and political liberalization. This liberalization process was not designed to generate a greater degree of political participation in existing governmental systems, but could simply mean any reform that enhanced the individual freedom of a citizen. Thus unlike Iraq and Iran, when it came to regimes such as Saudi Arabia, Egypt, Jordan, Kuwait, Morocco, and Yemen, the Bush administration did not advocate regime change through military action, democratic populism, or civil disobedience. That is to say, the Freedom Agenda recognized the growing potential for legitimation crises in the region, as identified by the 2002 *Arab Human Development Report* and attempted to prevent these crises. This demonstrates how the policy was unable to stave off such crises and exposed the region, in particular Tunisia and Egypt, to the 2008 global financial crisis. The conservative strand of the Freedom Agenda was designed to "slowly" transform the region in "partnership" with autocratic allies to avoid the scenes in Tunisia, Egypt, and Libya, and therefore not introduce the level of strategic uncertainty that the post-Tahrir Square era represents.[11]

Obama's Spring Time Policy: Moving Close to Europe

Upon coming into office it was clear that the Obama administration wanted to distance itself from the Freedom Agenda and its association with the Iraq war. President Obama was eager to suggest that the radical side of the Freedom Agenda would be replaced with a more pragmatic "open handed" approach. Moreover, many critics argued that the Obama administration seemed to abandon democracy promotion altogether because of its "toxic" associations with President Bush. Whilst Secretary of State Hillary Rodham Clinton was willing to assert the need for a "comprehensive plan" for "diplomacy, development, and defense," in her Senate confirmation hearing, "advancing democracy" was represented as a "hope."[12] On closer inspection, the Obama administration had expanded the conservative side of the Freedom Agenda through increased MEPI funding and the appointment of Tamara Coffman Wittes as Deputy Assistant Secretary for Near Eastern Affairs. Indeed, appointments such as Anne-Marie Slaughter to Director of Policy Planning, Susan Rice to UN Ambassador, and Samantha Power and Michael McFaul to the National Security Council, suggest that democracy promotion was clearly not removed from the Obama agenda.[13] The intellectual shift with their predecessors was most prominently demonstrated in the administration's emphasis on *dignity* and *development* as a means of countering Islamist organizations in the region and enabling a stable modernization process to take place. Thus, the language of "dignity and development" replaced talk of "democracy promotion," and the Obama administration initially attempted to replace "market driven modernization" with "development driven modernization" to underpin a gradualist strategy. However, in the aftermath of the 2011 revolutions the Obama administration increasingly came to see the Bush administration's approach as the preferred policy agenda.

On May 19, 2011, President Obama took center stage in the Department of State's Benjamin Franklin room to announce an apparently "bold new approach to foreign policy" and US relations with MENA.[14] He argued that the 2011 revolutions in MENA were caused by a denial of dignity, a lack of political and economic self-determination throughout the region, the role of new media, and the region's young demographic profile. He argued that Tunisia and Egypt were entering years of transition and that the process of transition would have ups and downs that would potentially challenge America's core interests, but that the administration would continue to "keep our commitments to friends and partners." Further echoing George W.

Bush, President Obama argued that the status quo was not sustainable and that the United States had a stake in the stability of nations and the self-determination of individuals in the region. As a result he reinforced the premises of Bush's liberal grand strategy for the Middle East, arguing that the United States should "not pursue the world as it is, but use this [the Arab Spring] as a chance to pursue the world as it should be."

In this context, the President began attempting to lay out his grand strategy for the region under the headings of political reform, human rights, and economic reform. He argued that since the Arab Spring, the United States had shown that it opposed the use of force and supported universal rights, as well as political and economic reform. The supposed new strategy would help support reform across the region starting in Tunisia and Egypt, while condemning partners such as Yemen and Bahrain for their use of force (and by implication Saudi Arabia). The president detailed how the United States would support change in the region through economic development to nations transitioning to democracy: America's support for democracy will therefore be built on financial stability, promoting reform, and integrating competitive markets with each other and with the global economy . . . starting with Tunisia and Egypt.

The President continued to argue that the problem with the region was its "closed economies" and that the region needed "trade," and "investment" and that "protectionism must give way to openness." Nonetheless, it was announced that:

- The World Bank and IMF were to construct a plan to present to the G8 Summit about what was needed to stabilize and modernize the economies of Tunisia and Egypt.
- Egypt would be relieved of $1 billion in debt.
- $1 billion in loans for infrastructure were allocated to Egypt.
- The United States would help to recover assets that were stolen.
- Enterprise Funds would be set up to invest in Tunisia and Egypt—modeled on the funds that helped democratic transition in Eastern Europe.

- OPEC would create a $2 billion facility to help support private investment.
- The United States would work with allies to re-focus the European Bank for reconstruction and development so it provided the same support for democratic transition and economic modernization in MENA as in Europe.
- Establish a comprehensive trade and investment initiative with MENA; working with the EU to facilitate more trade from within the region, and building on existing agreements to provide integration with the US and EU markets.
- Help these transition countries tear down the walls that stand in the way of progress and to fulfill their international obligations.

This was a very different understanding of the problem from that constructed by the protesters of Tahrir Square, where the concept of freedom was articulated with human rights, social justice, and in some significant quarters adherence to Islam.[15] Indeed, it would appear that rather than the Arab Spring and the global financial crisis occasioning America's democracy bureaucracy to pause for thought, they drew on their training in Eastern Europe to propose the "cookie cutter" approach of the Washington Consensus. The "new" policy is held together by a desire to hold onto the gradualist paradigm where possible, but where impossible to ensure that the opportunity of a crisis is not missed and free trade and the free market approach is adopted as the core of America's democracy promotion strategy. Notably, however, the Arab Spring has led the Obama administration to look towards closer cooperation with Europe and to further financial integration of MENA with the EU. In the past, the United States and the EU have always emphasized the importance of transatlantic "cooperation." For Bush's Freedom Agenda this was through the BMENA, and the Obama administration has continued to push for integration with US and EU markets. For the EU this is a welcome policy and helps fulfill the objectives of the European neighborhood policy. As other chapters in this volume demonstrate, European efforts to promote democracy in the region have been remarkably similar in their emphasis on partnership, gradualism, and economic liberalization. Given such similarities, and a certain level of cooperation between the transatlantic partners, the question remains whether America's decade-long effort to promote democracy in MENA provides important lessons for the EU, even if there is significant tension on the ground between EU delegations and US democracy promoters in the region itself.[16]

Lessons for European Cooperation?

Given the profound nature of the Arab Spring, which is radically transforming the region, it is problematic that there has not been a corresponding shift in the American democracy promotion policy. Indeed, the Obama administration bolted from their initial attempts to modify the policy and returned to the strategy set out by the Bush administration. This is not because the United States is pursuing sound policy programs, but on account of a lack of policy innovation within the Obama administration. US policy in the Middle East is in need of a new policy paradigm to replace those that failed. This is not easy because democratic transition in the region exacerbates a conflict of interest at the heart of US engagement with the region. This clearly presents a problem for the EU. Atlantic solidarity is moving European strategy towards a collaborative transatlantic partnership. This transatlantic approach defines "freedom" for the region in neo-liberal economic terms. This, however, is not just an economic strategy, but rather an imperial strategy where the United States and the EU attempt to socially engineer MENA societies through economic statecraft. Providing the region with a definition of freedom predominantly in economic terms is an attempt to create market democracies or, less euphemistically, low intensity democracy. This should be of the gravest concern to both the United States and the EU, who need to listen more closely to definitions of freedom and democracy emerging from the protesters on the street and the liberal and moderate movements within the region. If the United States and EU are to better understand how to engage with the region and create a new policy paradigm, they need to listen to the home-grown voices of Tahrir Square and to enter into a dialogue with *their* definitions of freedom and democracy, rather than impose a definition from outside. Within the EU this has been recognized at the delegation level, with EU officials on the ground looking for alternative strategies to those put forward by the United States, recognizing that collaboration with the United States may confuse the EU with a "toxic brand." Yet, with European policy largely predetermined in Brussels, and the promise of the Lisbon Treaty (whereby delegations on the ground make decisions) somewhat mythical, it appears that Europe will no doubt go down the wrong path along with its Atlantic partners.

This is all the more problematic because when listening to the protesters in Tahrir Square, it is clear that there are liberal voices present. When questioned about American policies in the region, they talk of the oppression brought to them through Western support for Mubarak, but hold America and Europe up as exemplars. Indeed, walking around Tahrir during the protest there were constant calls for "freedom"; talking to the organizers, they tell you how they studied the history of non-violent movements and cite amongst others Rosa Parks, Martin Luther King, and Malcolm X, before telling you how they studied what happened in Eastern Europe at the end of the Cold War. This is a definition of freedom that is based on a home-grown understanding of citizenship and social justice, articulated in a narrative that draws upon American and European history. American and European democracy promotion strategies need to grasp home-grown visions of the future if they are to construct a new policy paradigm and must move away from the democracy promotion strategies that so clearly failed over the last decade.

Notes

1. This acronym stands for *Advance Democratic Values, Address Non-democratic Countries, and Enhance Democracy Act*, passed as part of the Implementing Recommendations of the 9/11 Commission Act of 2007; H.R.1 Public Law 110–53, 22 USC 8201n; Title XXI, Sections 2101–62, as passed by the 110th Congress. President Bush ratified the bill on August 3, 2007.

2. Oz Hassan, *America's Freedom Agenda Towards the Middle East: Democracy or Domination* (London: Routledge, 2012).

3. Oz Hassan, "Bush's Freedom Agenda: Ideology and the Democratization of the Middle East," *Democracy and Security* 4, no. 3 (2008): 268–89.

4. "President Bush Discusses Freedom in Iraq and Middle East," last modified November 6, 2003, http://georgewbush-whitehouse.archives.gov/news/releases/2003/11/20031106-2.html.

5. Marina Ottaway, "The Problem of Credibility," in *Uncharted Journey: Promoting Democracy in the Middle East,* ed. Thomas Carothers and Marina Ottaway (Washington DC: Carnegie Endowment for International Peace, 2005), 182.

6. "U.S. Ideals Meet Reality in Yemen," *The Washington Post,* last modified September 23, 2009, http://www.washingtonpost.com/wp-dyn/content/article/2005/12/17/AR2005121701237_pf.html

7. Authors' interview with Tamara Coffman Wittes, Washington, D.C: Brookings Institution, July 2008.

8. "The National Security Strategy of the United States of America" accessed November 4, 2011, http://www.strategicstudiesinstitute.army.mil/pdffiles/nss.pdf.

9. "President Bush Presses for Peace in the Middle East," last modified May 9, 2003, http://georgewbush-whitehouse.archives.gov/news/releases/2003/05/20030509-11.html

10. Paul Magnusson, "A Man of Many Missions: Trade honcho Bob Zoellick has a strong diplomatic agenda," *Business Week*, 2003, 94.

11. Hassan, *America's Freedom Agenda Towards the Middle East.*

12. "Statement of Senator Hillary Rodham Clinton Nominee for Secretary of State," accessed November 4, 2011, http://foreign.senate.gov/testimony/2009/ClintonTestimony090113a.pdf

13. Nicolas Bouchet, "Barack Obama's democracy promotion at the midterm," *The International Journal of Human Rights* 15, no. 4 (2011): 572–88.

14. "Barack Obama's speech on Middle East—full transcript" last modified May, 19, 2011, http://www.guardian.co.uk/world/2011/may/19/barack-obama-speech-middle-east.

15. Author's ethnographic research in Tahrir Square, Cairo, Egypt, July-August 2011.

16. Author's anonymous research interviews in Cairo, Egypt, August 2011.

Bibliography

Abdullah, Daud. "Concerns about British and EU roles in Palestinian Authority Human Rights Abuses in the Occupied West Bank." CEO, Middle East Monitor, MEMO, London (2009): 1–19.

Al-Duraiby, Ibrahim Suleiman. *Saudi Arabia, GCC and the EU: Limitations and Possibilities for an Unequal Triangular Relationship*. Dubai: GRC Press, 2009.

Altunisik, Melhia Benli. "EU Foreign Policy and the Israeli-Palestinian Conflict: How Much of an Actor?" *European Security* 17, no. 1 (2008): 105–21.

Arendt, Hannah. *Edifier un monde: Interventions 1971–1975*. Translated by Mira Koller and Dominique Séglard. Paris: Editions du Seuil, 2007.

Baracani, Elena. "The European Neighbourhood Policy: A New Anchor for Conflict Settlement?" *Global Europe Papers* no. 2 (2008): 1–34.

Bellin, Eva. "The Robustness of Authoritarianism in the Middle East: Exceptionalism in Comparative Perspective." *Comparative Politics* 36, no. 2 (2004): 139–57.

Bicchi, Federica. "Our Size Fits All: Normative Power Europe and the Mediterranean." *Journal of European Public Policy* 13, no. 2 (2006): 286–303.

Bicchi, Federica, Laura Guazzone, and Daniela Pioppi, eds, La questione della democrazia nel mondo arabo: stati, società e conflitti. (Monza: Polimetrica, 2004).

Biscop, Sven. "Mayhem in the Mediterranean: Three Strategic Lessons for Europe." Egmont, Royal Institute for International Relations, Security Policy Brief No. 19 (April 2011). Accessed October 17, 2011, http://www.egmontinstitute.be/papers/11/sec-gov/SPB19-Libya-strat-lessons-EU.pdf

Blockmans, Steven, and Ramses A. Wessel. "The European Union and Crisis Management: Will the Lisbon Treaty Make the EU More Effective?" *Journal of Conflict & Security Law* 14, no. 2 (2009): 265–308.

Bouchet, Nicolas. "Barack Obama's Democracy Promotion at the Midterm." *The International Journal of Human Rights* 15, no. 4 (2011): 572–88.

Cassarino, Jean-Pierre. "The EU-Tunisian Association Agreement and Tunisia's Structural Reform Program." *Middle East Journal* 53, no. 1 (1999): 59–74.

Cassarino, Jean-Pierre, ed. *Unbalanced Reciprocities: Cooperation on Readmission in the Euro-Mediterranean Area.* Washington, D.C.: The Middle East Institute, 2010.

Challand, Benoît. "The Arab Revolts and the Cage of Political Economy." *Insurgent Notes: Journal Of Communist Theory and Practise,* no 4. (2011): 128–47.

Council of the European Union. "A Secure Europe in a Better World: The European Security Strategy", Brussels, December 12, 2003. Accessed October 17, 2011. http://www.consilium.europa.eu/uedocs/cmsUpload/78367.pdf

Crawford, Gordon. "Foreign Aid and Political Conditionality: Issues of Effectiveness and Consistency." *Democratization* 4 no. 3 (1997): 69–108.

———. *Foreign Aid and Political Reform: A Comparative Analysis of Democracy Assistance and Political Conditionality.* Basingstoke: Palgrave, 2001.

Del Sarto, Raffaella, and Tobias Schumacher. "From Brussels with Love: Leverage, Benchmarking, and the Action Plans with Jordan and Tunisia in the EU's Democratization Policy." *Democratization* 18, no. 4 (2011): 932–56.

Del Sarto, Raffaella, and Tobias Schumacher, Erwan Lannon, Ahmed Driss. "Benchmarking Democratic Development in the Euro-Mediterranean Area: Conceptualising Ends, Means and Strategies." *EuroMeSCOAnnual Report 2006.* Lisbon: EUROMESCO, 2007.

Del Sarto, Raffaella. "Wording and Meaning(s): EU-Israeli Political Cooperation according to the ENP Action Plan" *Mediterranean Politics* 11, 1 (2007): 59–74.

Duke, Simon, and Hanna Ojanen. "Bridging Internal and External Security: Lessons from the European Security and Defence Policy." *European Integration* 28, no. 5 (2006): 477–94.

Echagüe, Ana. "The European Union and the Gulf Cooperation Council." *FRIDE Working Paper* 39 (2007).

Emerson, Michael. "Review of the Review of the European Neighbourhood Policy." *Centre for European Policy Studies* 1 (2011).

Euro-Mediterranean Human Rights Network. "Freedom of Association and Human Rights Organizations in Egypt." Accessed October 23, 2011. http://www.euromedrights.org/en/publications-en/emhrn-publications/emhrn-publications 1999/3588.html.

European Commission. "The European Union and the External Dimension of Human Rights Policy: From Rome to Maastricht and Beyond," COM/95/567 final. Brussels: 22 November 1995.

———. "Reinvigorating the Barcelona Process," COM(2000) 297 final. Brussels: 6 October 2000.

———. "Reinvigorating EU Actions on Human Rights and Democratisation with Mediterranean Partners - Strategic Guidelines," COM(2003) 294 final. Brussels: 21 May 2003.

———. "Communication from the Commission to the Council on the Commission Proposals for Action Plans under the European Neighbourhood Policy (ENP)," COM(2004) 795 final. Brussels: 9 December 2004.

———. "EU-Egypt Action Plan." Accessed October 23, 2011. http://trade.ec.europa.eu/doclib/docs/2010/april/tradoc_146097.pdf.

———. "A Partnership for Democracy and Shared Prosperity with the Southern Mediterranean," COM(2011) 200 final. Brussels, 8 March 2011.

European Commission and High Representative. "A New Response to a Changing Neighbourhood," COM(2011) 303 final. Brussels: 25 May 2011.

Fioramonti, Lorenzo. *European Union Democracy Aid: Supporting Civil Society in Post-Apartheid South Africa*. London: Routledge, 2010.

Friedrich, Roland, and Arnold Luethold. "And They Came in and Took Possession of Reforms: Ownership and Palestinian SSR." In *Local Ownership and Security Sector Reform*, 191–213. Geneva: Centre for the Democratic Control of Armed Forces (DCAF), 2008.

Hassan, Oz. *America's Freedom Agenda Towards the Middle East: Democracy or Domination*. London: Routledge, 2012.

———. "Bush's Freedom Agenda: Ideology and the Democratization of the Middle East," *Democracy and Security* 4, no. 3 (2008): 268–89.

Held, David. *Democracy and the Global Order: From the Modern State to Cosmopolitan Governance*. Cambridge: Polity Press, 1995.

Hibou, Béatrice. *La Force de l'obéissance: Economie politique de la répression en Tunisie*. Paris: La Découverte, 2006.

Hollis, Rosemary. "The UfM and the Middle East 'Peace Process': An Unhappy Symbiosis." *Mediterranean Politics* 16, no. 1 (2011): 99–116.

Human Rights Watch. "World Report 2011: Egypt." Accessed October 23, 2011. http://www.hrw.org/en/world-report-2011/egypt.

Human Rights Watch. "World Report 2011: Tunisia." Accessed 17 October, 2011. http://www.hrw.org/world-report-2011/tunisia.

Jung, Dietrich. "Unrest in the Arab World: Four Questions." *Insight Turkey* 13, no. 3 (2011):1–10.

Kaldor, Mary, et al. *A Human Security Doctrine for Europe: The Barcelona Report of the Study Group on Europe's Security Capabilities*.

———. *Human Security: Reflections on Globalization*. Cambridge: Polity Press, 2007.

Keukelerie, Stephan, and Jennifer MacNaughtan. *The Foreign Policy of the European Union*. Basingstoke: Palgrave/Macmillan, 2008.

Kirchner, Emile J. "EU Security Governance in a Wider Europe." In *Managing a Multilevel Foreign Policy*, edited by P. Foradori, P. Rosa, and R. Scartezzini, 23–41. New York: Rowman & Littlefield Publishers, 2007.

Light, Margot, and Karen Smith, eds. *Ethics and Foreign Policy*. Cambridge: Cambridge University Press, 2001.

Leenders, Reinoud and Eva Goes. "Promoting Democracy and Human Rights in Lebanon and Syria." In *Crescent of Crisis. U.S.-European Strategy for the Greater Middle East*, edited by Ivo Daalder, Nicole Gnesotto, and Philip Gordon, 94–109. Washington, D.C.: The Brookings Institution, 2006.

Lucarelli, Sonia, and Ian Manners, eds. *Values and Principles in European Union Foreign Policy*. London and New York: Routledge, 2006.

Luciani, Giacomo, and Tobias Schumacher. *Relations Between the European Union and the Gulf Cooperation Council States. Past Record and Promises for the Future*. Dubai: GRC Press, 2004.

Manners, Ian. "Normative Power Europe: A Contradiction in Terms?" *Journal of Common Market Studies* 40, no. 2 (2002): 235–58.

Møller, Bjørn. "The EU as a Security Actor: 'Security by Being' and 'Security by Doing.'" Danish Institute for International Studies (DIIS) Report 2005:12, Copenhagen (2005): 1–76.

Murphy, Emma C. "The Tunisian *Mise à Niveau* Programme and the Political Economy of Reform." *New Political Economy* 11, no. 4 (2006): 519–40.

Pace, Michelle. "The EU and the Mediterranean." In *The European Union and Global Governance: A Handbook*, edited by David J. Bailey and Jens-Uwe Wunderlich, 304–312. London: Routledge, 2011.

Pardo, Sharon, and Joel Peters. *Uneasy Neighbors: Israel and the European Union*. Lanham, MD: Lexington Books, 2010.

———. *Israel and the European Union: A Documentary History*. Lanham, MD: Lexington Books, 2011.

O'Donnell, Clara. *The EU, Israel and Hamas*. Centre for European Reform Working Paper, (2008). Accessed on November 7, 2001, http://www.cer.org.uk/sites/default/files/publications/.../wp_820-1475.pdf.

Olsen, Gorm Rye. "Europe and the Promotion of Democracy in Post Cold War Africa: How Serious Is Europe and For What Reason?" *African Affairs* 97, no. 388 (1998): 343–67.

———. "Promotion of Democracy as a Foreign Policy Instrument of 'Europe': Limits to International Idealism." *Democratization* 7, no. 2 (2000): 142–67.

Ottaway, Marina. "The Problem of Credibility." In *Uncharted Journey: Promoting Democracy in the Middle East*, edited by Thomas Carothers and Marina Ottaway, 173–92. Washington, D.C.: Carnegie Endowment for International Peace, 2005.

Sayigh, Yezid. "Inducing a Failed State in Palestine." *Survival* 49, no. 3 (2007): 7–39.

———. "'Fixing Broken Windows': Security Sector Reform in Palestine, Lebanon, and Yemen." *Carnegie Papers* no. 17, Carnegie Endowment for International Peace (2009): 1–36.

Schlumberger, Oliver, ed. *Debating Arab Authoritarianism. Dynamics and Durability in Non-Democratic Regimes*. Stanford: Stanford University Press, 2009.

Schulz, Michael. "The European Union as Third Party in the Israeli-Palestinian Conflict." In *War and Peace in Transition: Changing Roles and Practices of External Actors*, edited by Karin Aggestam and Annika Björkdahl, 72–89. Lund: Nordic Academic Press, 2009.

Schumacher, Tobais. "The EU and the Arab Spring: Between Spectatorship and Actorness." *Insight Turkey* 13, no. 3 (2011): 107–20.

———. *Transatlantic Cooperation in the Middle East and North Africa and the Growing Role of the Gulf States*. Washington: The German Marshall Fund of the United States, 2010.

Seeberg, Peter. "The EU as a Realist Actor in Normative Clothes: EU Democracy Promotion in Lebanon and the European Neighborhood Policy." *Democratization* 16, no. 1 (2008): 81–99.

Sherriff, Andrew. "Security Sector Reform and EU Norm Implementation." In *Intergovernmental Organisations and Security Sector Reform*, edited by David Law, 85–102. Geneva: Centre for the Democratic Control of Armed Forces, 2007.

Smith, Karen E. "The Use of Political Conditionality in the EU's Relations with Third Countries: How Effective?" *European Foreign Affairs Review* 3, no. 2 (1998): 253–74.

Söderbaum, Fredrik, and Patrik Stålgren, eds. *The European Union and the Global South*. Boulder: Lynne Rienner Publishers, 2010.

Tavares, Rodrigo. *Regional Security: The Capacity of International Organizations*. New York: Routledge, 2010.

Tocci, Nathalie. "The Impact of Western Policies towards Hamas and Hezbollah: What Went Wrong?" In *Political Islam and European Foreign Policy. Perspectives from Muslim Democrats of the Mediterranean*, edited by Michael Emerson and Richard Youngs, 136–75. Brussels: Centre for European Policy Studies, 2007.

———. *The EU and Conflict Resolution: Promoting Peace in the Backyard*. London: Routledge, 2007.

Wittes, Tamara Cofman, and Richard Youngs. "Europe, the United States, and Middle Eastern Democracy: Repairing the Breach." The Saban Center for Middle East Policy at the Brookings University, Analysis Paper 18 (2009).

Youngs, Richard. "Impasse in Euro-Gulf Relations." FRIDE Working Paper 80 (April 2009).

———. "Democracy Promotion: The Case of the European Union Strategy." *CEPS Working Document*, no.167, 2001.

———. "The European Union and Democracy Promotion in the Mediterranean: A New or Disingenuous Strategy?" In *European Union and Democracy Promotion: the Case of North Africa*, edited by R. Gillespie and Richard Youngs, special issue of *Democratization* 9, no. 1 (2002): 40–62.

Zorob, Anja. "Partnership with the European Union: Hopes, Risks and Challenges for the Syrian Economy." In *Demystifying Syria*, edited by Fred H. Lawson, 144–158. London: SOAS, 2009.

Index

About the Contributors

Carin Berg is a PhD student in Peace and Development Research at the School of Global Studies at the University of Gothenburg, Sweden. She has lived and worked in several countries in the Middle East and has published about different issues concerning the Middle East, and in particular the Israeli-Palestinian Conflict.

Jean-Pierre Cassarino is professor at the Robert Schuman Centre for Advanced Studies (RSCAS, European University Institute, Florence, Italy). He is also associate researcher at the Institut de Recherche sur le Maghreb Contemporain (IRMC, Tunis). He has published extensively on political and economic reforms in North African countries and on the cooperation on migration and border controls in Euro-Arab bilateral and multilateral talks.

Lorenzo Fioramonti is associate professor of political science at the University of Pretoria, where he coordinates the Research Unit for Euro-African Studies. He is also Senior Fellow at the University of Bologna (Italy), at the University of Heidelberg, and at the Hertie School of Governance (Germany). His most recent publications include *Regions and Crises*, *Regionalism in a Changing World*, *European Union Democracy Aid*, and *External Perceptions of the European Union as a Global Actor*.

Oz Hassan is a senior research fellow in the Centre for the Study of Globalisation and Regionalisation at the University of Warwick. He is the author of *America's Freedom Agenda towards the Middle East* in the Routledge Studies in US Foreign Policy Series, edited a special issue of the *International Journal of Human Rights* focusing on democracy promotion, and authored several related journal articles on US and EU policy in the Middle East and North Africa. He has conducted ethnographic research in the Middle East, and witnessed first hand the protestor struggles in Cairo's Tahrir Square following the fall of the Mubarak regime.

Michelle Pace is reader in politics and international studies at the Department of Political Science and International Studies, University of Birmingham, UK. She is also principal investigator on an Economic and Social Research Council Large First Grant Scheme research project on Paradoxes and Contradictions in EU Democracy Promotion Efforts in the Middle East. Her publications include: *Europe, the USA and Political Islam: Strategies for Engagement*, and (with Peter Seeberg) *The European Union's Democratization Agenda in the Mediterranean*.

Joel Peters is associate professor of government and international affairs in the School of Public and International Affairs at Virginia Tech. He was previously the founding director of the Centre for the Study of Israeli Politics and Society at Ben Gurion University, Israel. He is the author (with Sharon Pardo) of *Uneasy Neighbors: Israel and the European Union* and *Israel and the European Union: A Documentary History*, and co-editor (with David Newman) of the *Routledge Handbook on the Israeli-Palestinian Conflict* (forthcoming), as well as numerous articles on the EU and the Israeli-Palestinian conflict.

Marco Pinfari is fellow in global politics at the Department of Government and the Department of International Relations at the London School of Economics and Political Science. He published widely in conflict analysis in journals such as the *Journal of Conflict Resolution* and *Terrorism and Political Violence*. His recent publications include "Europe and Conflict Resolution in the Mediterranean: The Impact of Hybrid Wars" and "Nothing but Failure? The Arab League and the Gulf Cooperation Council as Mediators in Middle Eastern Conflicts" (Crisis States Working Papers Series). In 2010 he was visiting lecturer at the EuroMed Masters and PhD programme at Cairo University, Egypt.

Michael Schulz is associate professor in Peace and Development Research at the School of Global Studies at the University of Gothenburg, Sweden. His most recent publications are "Palestinian public willingness to compromise: torn between hope and violence" (*Journal of Security Dialogue*) and "The role of civil society in regional governance in the Middle East" in Valeria Bello, Cristiano Bee, and David Armstrong (eds.), *Civil Society and International Governance*.

Tobias Schumacher is senior researcher in political science at the Centre for Research and Studies in Sociology (CIES) at the Lisbon University Institute (ISCTE-IUL), Portugal. He has published numerous books and articles on EU external relations, Euro-Mediterranean relations, Middle East and North Africa politics, and in the field of foreign policy analysis and political economy. Among his latest publications are: "From Brussels with Love: Leverage, Benchmarking, and the Action Plans with Jordan and Tunisia in the EU's Democratization Policy" (with Raffaella Del Sarto), in *Democratization* 18(4), 2011 and "The EU and the Arab Spring: Between Spectatorship and Actorness," in *Insight Turkey* 13(3), 2011, and "Conditionality, Differentiation, Regionality and the 'New' ENP in the Light of Arab Revolts," in Esther Barbé und Anna Herranz-Surrallés (Hrsg.), *Differentiation in Euro-Mediterranean Relations. Towards Flexible Region Building or Fragmentation?*, London: Routledge, 2012.

CPSIA information can be obtained at www.ICGtesting.com
Printed in the USA
BVOW042150030612

291597BV00001B/3/P